RUTH FIELDING IN THE GREAT NORTHWEST

OR, THE INDIAN GIRL STAR OF THE MOVIES

ALICE B. EMERSON

1st WORLD LIBRARY
Literary Society

Ruth Fielding in the Great Northwest

Alice B. Emerson

© 1st World Library, 2007
PO Box 2211
Fairfield, IA 52556
www.1stworldlibrary.com
First Edition

LCCN: 2007930754

Softcover ISBN: 978-1-4218-4786-3
Hardcover ISBN: 978-1-4218-4689-7
eBook ISBN: 978-1-4218-4883-9

Purchase *"Ruth Fielding in the Great Northwest"*
as a traditional bound book at:
www.1stWorldLibrary.com/purchase.asp?ISBN= 978-1-4218-4786-3

1st World Library is a literary, educational organization
dedicated to:

- Creating a free internet library of downloadable ebooks

- Hosting writing competitions and offering book publishing
  scholarships.

Interested in more 1st World Library books? contact:
literacy@1stworldlibrary.com
Check us out at: www.1stworldlibrary.com

1ˢᵗ World Library Literary Society

Giving Back to the World

"If you want to work on the core problem, it's early school literacy."
                                    - James Barksdale, former CEO of Netscape

"No skill is more crucial to the future of a child, or to a democratic and prosperous society, than literacy."

                                                        - Los Angeles Times

"Literacy... means far more than learning how to read and write... The aim is to transmit... knowledge and promote social participation."
                                                        - UNESCO

"Literacy is not a luxury, it is a right and a responsibility. If our world is to meet the challenges of the twenty-first century we must harness the energy and creativity of all our citizens."

                                                - President Bill Clinton

"Parents should be encouraged to read to their children, and teachers should be equipped with all available techniques for teaching literacy, so the varying needs and capacities of individual kids can be taken into account."
                                                        - Hugh Mackay

CONTENTS

I. RUTH IN PERIL 7

II. A PERFECT SHOT...14

III. IN THE RING..21

IV. SMOKING THE PEACE PIPE 28

V. INSPIRATION..35

VI. EVERYBODY AGREES BUT DAKOTA JOE...............43

VII. DAKOTA JOE'S WRATH....................................49

VIII. A WONDERFUL EVENT...................................56

IX. THE PLOT DEVELOPS 61

X. ONE NEW YORK DAY 69

XI. EVADING THE TRAFFIC POLICE 80

XII. BOUND FOR THE NORTHWEST.....................86

XIII. DAKOTA JOE MAKES A DEMAND...........................93

XIV. THE HUBBELL RANCH 100

XV. PURSUING DANGER 108

XVI. NEWS AND A THREAT............................... 115

XVII. THE PROLOGUE IS FINISHED 122

XVIII. AN ACCIDENT THREATENING.................. 128

XIX. IN DEADLY PERIL..................................... 134

XX. GOOD NEWS 139

XXI. A BULL AND A BEAR 146

XXII. IN THE CANYON 152

XXIII. REALITY... 159

XXIV. WONOTA'S SURPRISE 166

XXV. OTHER SURPRISES................................. 171

CHAPTER I

RUTH IN PERIL

The gray dust, spurting from beneath the treads of the rapidly turning wheels, drifted across the country road to settle on the wayside hedges. The purring of the engine of Helen Cameron's car betrayed the fact that it was tuned to perfection. If there were any rough spots in the road being traveled, the shock absorbers took care of them.

"Dear me! I always do love to ride in Nell's car," said the plump and pretty girl who occupied more than her share of the rear seat. "Even if Tom isn't here to take care of it, it always is so comfy."

"Only one thing would suit you better, Heavy," declared the sharp-featured and sharp-tongued girl sitting next to Jennie Stone. "If only a motor could be connected to a rocking-chair—"

"Right-o!" agreed the cheerful plump girl. "And have it on a nice shady porch. I'd like to travel that way just as well. After our experience in France we ought to be allowed to travel in comfort for the rest of our lives. Isn't that so, Nell? And you agree, Ruthie?"

The girl at the wheel of the flying automobile nodded only,

for she needed to keep her gaze fixed ahead. But the brown-haired, brown-eyed girl, whose quiet face seemed rather wistful, turned to smile upon the volatile—and voluble—Heavy Stone, so nicknamed during their early school days at Briarwood Hall.

"Don't let's talk about it, honey," she said. "I try not to think of what we all went through."

"And the soup I tasted!" groaned the plump one. "That diet kitchen in Paris! I'll never get over it—never!"

"I guess *that's* right," agreed Mercy Curtis, the sharp-featured girl. "How that really nice Frenchman can stand for such a fat girl—"

"Why," explained Heavy calmly, "the more there is of me the more there is for him to like." Then she giggled. "There were so few fat people left in Europe after four years of war that everybody liked to look at me."

"You certainly are a sight for sore eyes," Helen Cameron shot over her shoulder, but without losing sight of the road ahead. She was a careful, if rapid, driver. "And for any other eyes! One couldn't very well miss you, Heavy."

"Let's not talk any more about France—or the war—or anything like that," proposed Ruth Fielding, the shadow on her face deepening. "Both your Henri and Helen's Tom have had to go back—"

"Helen's Tom?" repeated Mercy Curtis softly. But Jennie Stone pinched her. She would not allow anybody to tease Ruth, although they all knew well enough that the absence of Helen's twin brother meant as much to Ruth Fielding as it did to his sister.

　　　　　　　Alice B. Emerson

This was strictly a girl's party, this ride in Helen Cameron's automobile. Aside from Mercy, who was the daughter of the Cheslow railroad station agent, and therefore lived in Cheslow all the year around, the girls were not native to the place. They had just left that pretty town behind them. It appeared that Ruth, Helen, and surely Jennie Stone, knew very few of the young men of Cheslow. So this jaunt was, as Jennie saucily said, entirely "*poulette*".

"Which she thinks is French for 'old hen,'" scoffed the tart Mercy.

"I do not know which is worse," Ruth Fielding said with a sigh, as Helen slowed down for a railroad crossing at which stood a flagman. "Heavy's French or her slang."

"Slang! Never!" cried the plump girl, tossing her head "Far be it from me and et cetera. I never use slang. I am quite as much of a purist as that professor at Ardmore—what was his name?—that they tell the story about. The dear dean told him that some of the undergrads complained that his language was 'too pedantic and unintelligible.'"

"'Never, Madam! Impossible! Why,' said the prof, 'to employ a vulgarism, perspicuity is my penultimate appellative.'"

"Ow! Ow!" groaned Helen at the wheel "I bet that hurt your vocal cords, Heavy."

She let in the clutch again as the party broke into laughter, and they darted across the tracks behind the passing train.

"Just the same," added Helen, "I wish some of the boys we used to play around with were with us. Those fellows Tom went to Seven Oaks with were all nice boys. Dear me!"

"Most of them went into the war," Ruth reminded her.

"Nothing is as it used to be. Oh, dear!"

"I must say you are all very cheerful—not!" exclaimed Jennie. "Ruth is a regular Grandmother Grimalkin, and the rest of you are little better. I for one just won't think of my dear Henri as being food for cannon. I just won't! Why! before he and Tom can get into the nasty business again the war may be over. Just see the reports in the papers of what our boys are doing. They really have the Heinies on the run."

"Ye-as," murmured Mercy. "Running which way?"

"Treason!" cried Jennie. "The only way the Germans have ever run forward is by crawling."

"Oh! Oh! Listen to the Irish bull!" cried Helen.

"Oh, is it?" exclaimed Jennie. "Maybe there is a bit of Irish in the McStones, or O'Stones. I don't know."

She certainly was the life of the party. Helen and Ruth had too recently bidden Tom Cameron good-bye to feel like joining with Jennie in repartee. Though it might have been that even the fat girl's repartee was more a matter of repertoire. She was expected to be funny, and so forced herself to make good her reputation.

This trip by automobile in fact was a forced attempt to cheer each other up on the part of the chums. At the Outlook, the Cameron's handsome country home, matters had become quite too awful to contemplate with calm, now that Tom had gone back to France. At least, so Helen stated. At the Red Mill Ruth had been (she admitted it) ready to "fly to pieces." For naturally poor Aunt Alvirah and Jabez Potter, the miller, were pot cheerful companions. And the two chums had Jennie Stone as their guest, for she had returned from New York with them, where they had all gone to bid Tom and

Henri Marchand farewell.

The three college friends had picked Mercy Curtis up (she had been with them at boarding-school "years and years before," to quote Jennie) and started on this trip from Cheslow to Longhaven. On the outskirts of Longhaven a Wild West Show was advertised as having pitched its tents.

"And, of course, if there is anything about the Wild West close at hand our movie writer must see it," said Jennie. "Give you local color, Ruth, for another western screen masterpiece."

"I suppose it is one of these little fly-by-night shows!" scoffed Mercy. "Let's see that bill. Dakota Joe's Wild West and Frontier Round-Up' Mm! Sounds big. But the bigger they sound the smaller they are, as a rule."

"I am glad I am not a pessimist," sighed Jennie Stone. "It must be an awfully uncomfortable feeling inside one to wear such a cloak."

"Ow! Ow!" cried Helen again. "Another Hibernianism, without a doubt."

She turned the car into a much-traveled road just then. Not a mile ahead loomed the "big top." A band was playing, and what it lacked in sweetness it certainly made up in noise.

"Look at the cars!" exclaimed Ruth, becoming interested. "We shall have to park before long, Helen, and walk to the show lot."

"Right here!" returned Helen, with vigor, and turned her car into a field where already a dozen automobiles were parked. A man with a whisp of whisker on his chin, and actually chewing a straw, motioned the young girl where to run her car. He was evidently the farmer who owned the field, and he was surely "making hay while the sun shone," for he was collecting a quarter from every automobile owner who wished to get his car off the public road.

"Your car'll be all right here, young ladies," he said, reaching for the quarter Ruth offered him. "I'm going to stay here myself and watch 'em until the show's over. Cal'late to stay here anyway till them wild Injuns and wilder cowboys air off Peleg Swift's land yonder. No knowing what they'll do if they ain't watched."

"Listen to the opinion our friend has of your old Wild West Show," hissed Jennie, as Ruth hopped out of the seat beside Helen.

Ruth laughed. The other girls, getting out of the car on the other side, were startled by hearing her laugh change to a sudden ejaculation.

"Dear me! has that thing broken loose from the show?"

Jennie was the first to speak, and she stepped behind the high car in order to catch sight of what had caused Ruth's exclamation. Instantly the plump girl emitted a most unseemly shout:

"Oh! Oh! Look at the bull!"

"What is the matter with you, Heavy?" demanded Mercy snappishly.

But when she and Helen followed the plump girl behind the automobile, they were stricken dumb with amazement, if not with fear. Tearing down the field toward the row of automobiles was a big black bull—head down, strings of foam flying from his mouth, and with every other indication

Alice B. Emerson

of extreme wrath.

"Run!" shrieked Jennie, and turned to do so.

She bumped into Mercy and Helen, who clung to her and really retarded the plump girl's escape. But plowing right on to the shelter of the automobile, Jennie actually swept her two friends with her.

Their cries and evident fright attracted the notice of the farmer before he really knew what was happening. Then he saw the bull and gave tongue to his own immediate excitement:

"Look at that critter! He's broke out of the barnyard—drat him! Don't let him see you, gals, for he's as vicious as sin!"

He started forward with a stick in his hand to attack the enraged bull. But the animal paid no attention to him. It had set its eyes upon something which excited its rage—Ruth Fielding's red sweater!

"Oh, Ruth! Ruth!" shrieked Helen, suddenly seeing her chum cornered on the other side of the car.

Ruth tried to open the car door again. But it stuck. Nor was there time for the girl of the Red Mill to vault the door and so escape the charge of the maddened bull. The brute was upon her.

CHAPTER II

A PERFECT SHOT

One may endure dangers of divers kinds (and Ruth Fielding had done so by land and sea) and be struck down unhappily by an apparently ordinary peril. The threat of that black bull's charge was as poignant as anything that had heretofore happened to the girl of the Red Mill.

After that first outcry, Ruth did not raise her voice at all. She tugged at the fouled handle of the automobile door, looking back over her shoulder at the forefront of the bull. He bellowed, and the very sound seemed to weaken her knees. Had she not been clinging to that handle she must have dropped to the earth.

And then, Crack! It was unmistakably a rifle shot.

The bull plowed up several yards of sod, swerved, shook his great head, bellowing again, and then started off at a tangent across the field with the farmer, brandishing a stick, close on his heels.

Saved, Ruth Fielding did sink to the earth now, and when the other girls ran clamorously around the motor-car she was scarcely possessed of her senses. Truly, however, she had been through too many exciting events to be long overcome

Alice B. Emerson

by this one.

Many queer experiences and perilous adventures had come into Ruth Fielding's life since the time when, as an orphan of twelve years, she had come to the Red Mill, just outside the town of Cheslow, to live with her Great Uncle Jabez and his queer little old housekeeper, Aunt Alvirah.

The miller was not the man generously to offer Ruth the advantages she craved. Had it not been for her dearest friend, Helen Cameron, at first Ruth would not have been dressed well enough to enter the local school. But if Jabez Potter was a miser, he was a just man after his fashion. Ruth saved him a considerable sum of money during the first few months of her sojourn at the Red Mill, and in payment for this Uncle Jabez allowed her to accompany Helen Cameron to that famous boarding school, Briarwood Hall.

While at school at Briarwood, and during the vacations between semesters, Ruth Fielding's career actually began, as the volumes following "Ruth Fielding of the Red Mill" show. The girl had numerous adventures at Briarwood Hall, at Snow Camp, at Lighthouse Point, at Silver Ranch, on Cliff Island, at Sunrise Farm, among the gypsies, in moving pictures, down in Dixie, at college, in the saddle, in the Red Cross in France, at the war front, and when homeward bound. The volume just previous to this present story related Ruth's adventures "Down East," where she went with Helen and Tom Cameron, as well as Jennie Stone, Jennie's fiance, Henri Marchand, and her Aunt Kate, who was their chaperon.

The girl of the Red Mill had long before the time of the present narrative proved her talent as a scenario writer, and working for Mr. Hammond, president of the Alectrion Film Corporation, had already made several very successful pictures. It seemed that her work in life was to be connected with the silver sheet.

Even Uncle Jabez had acknowledged Ruth's ability as a scenario writer, and was immensely proud of her work when he learned how much money she was making out of the pictures. For the old miller judged everything by a monetary standard.

Aunt Alvirah was, of course, very proud of her "pretty" as she called Ruth Fielding. Indeed, all Ruth's friends considered her success in picture-making as only going to show just how smart Ruth Fielding was. But the girl of the Red Mill was far too sensible to have her head turned by such praise. Even Tom Cameron's pride in her pictures only made the girl glad that she succeeded in delighting him.

For Ruth and Tom were closer friends now than ever before—and for years they had been "chummy." The adventures which had thrown them so much together in France while Tom was a captain in the American Expeditionary Forces and Ruth was working with the American Red Cross, had welded their confidence in and liking for each other until it seemed that nothing but their youth and Tom's duties in the army kept them from announcing their engagement.

"Do finish the war quickly, Tom," she had said to him whimsically, not long before Tom had gone back to France. "I do not feel as though I could return to college, or write another scenario, or do another single solitary thing until peace is declared."

"And *then*?" Tom had asked significantly, and Ruth had given him an understanding smile.

The uncertainty of that time—the whole nation waited and listened breathlessly for news from abroad—seemed to Ruth more than she could bear. She had entered upon this pleasure

Alice B. Emerson

jaunt to the Wild West Show with the other girls because she knew that anything to take their minds off the more serious thoughts of the war was a good thing.

Now, as she felt herself in peril of being gored by that black bull a tiny thought flashed into her mind:

"What terrible peril may be facing Tom Cameron at this identical moment?"

When the bull was gone, wounded by that unexpected rifle shot, and her three chums gathered about her, this thought of Tom's danger was still uppermost in Ruth's mind.

"Dear me, how silly of me!" she murmured. "There are lots worse things happening every moment over there than being gored by a bull."

"What an idea!" ejaculated Helen. "Are you crazy? What has that to do with you being pitched over that fence, for instance?"

She glanced at the fence which divided the field in which the automobiles stood from that where the two great tents of the Wild West Show were pitched. A broad-hatted man was standing at the bars. He drawled:

"Gal ain't hurt none, is she? That was a close shave—closer, a pile, than I'd want to have myself. Some savage critter, that bull. And if Dakota Joe's gal wasn't a crack shot that young lady would sure been throwed higher than Haman."

Ruth had now struggled to her feet with the aid of Jenny and Mercy.

"Do find out who it was shot the bull!" she cried.

Jennie, although still white-faced, grinned broadly again. "*Now* who is guilty of the most atrocious slang? 'Shot the bull,' indeed!"

"Thar she is," answered the broad-hatted man, pointing to a figure approaching the fence. Helen fairly gasped at sight of her.

"Right out of a Remington black-and-white," she shrilled in Ruth Fielding's ear.

The sight actually jolted Ruth's mind away from the fright which had overwhelmed it. She stared at the person indicated with growing interest as well as appreciation of the picturesque figure she made. She was an Indian girl in the gala costume of her tribe, feather head-dress and all. Or, perhaps, one would better say she was dressed as the white man expects an Indian to dress when on exhibition.

But aside from her dress, which was most attractive, the girl herself held Ruth's keen interest. Despite her high cheek-bones and the dusky copper color of her skin, this strange girl's features were handsome. There was pride expressed in them—pride and firmness and, withal, a certain sadness that added not a little to the charm of the Indian girl's visage.

"What a strange person!" murmured Helen Cameron.

"She is pretty," announced the assured Mercy Curtis, who always held her own opinion to be right on any subject. "One brunette never does like another," and she made a little face at Helen.

"Listen!" commanded Jennie Stone. "What does she say?"

The Indian girl spoke again, and this time they all heard her.

Alice B. Emerson

"Is the white lady injured, Conlon?"

"No, ma'am!" declared the broad-hatted man. "She'll be as chipper as a blue-jay in a minute. That was a near shot, Wonota. For an Injun you're some shot, I'll tell the world."

An expression of disdain passed over the Indian girl's face. She looked away from the man and Ruth's glance caught her attention.

"I thank you very much, Miss—Miss—"

"I am called Wonota in the Osage tongue," interposed the Indian maiden composedly enough.

"She's Dakota Joe's Injun sharpshooter," put in the man at the fence. "And she ain't no business out here in her play-actin' costume—or with her gun loaded that-a-way. Aginst the law. That gun she uses is for shootin' glass balls and clay pigeons in the show."

"Well, Miss Wonota," said Ruth, trying to ignore the officious man who evidently annoyed the Indian maiden, "I am very thankful you did have your rifle with you at this particular juncture." She approached the fence and reached over it to clasp the Indian girl's hand warmly.

"We are going in to see you shoot at the glass balls, for I see the show is about to start. But afterward, Wonota, can't we see you again?"

The Indian girl's expression betrayed some faint surprise. But she bowed gravely.

"If the white ladies desire," she said. "I must appear now in the tent. The boss is strict."

"You bet he is," added the broad-hatted man, who seemed offensively determined to push himself forward.

"After the show, then," said Ruth promptly to the girl. "I will tell you then just how much obliged to you I am," and she smiled in a most friendly fashion.

Wonota's smile was faint, but her black eyes seemed suddenly to sparkle. The man at the fence looked suspiciously from the white girls to the Indian maid, but he made no further comment as Wonota hastened away.

Alice B. Emerson

CHAPTER III

IN THE RING

"What do you know about that Indian girl?" demanded Jennie Stone excitedly. "She was just as cool as a cucumber. Think of her shooting that bull just in the nick of time and saving our Ruth!"

"It does seem," remarked Mercy Curtis in her sharp way, "that Ruthie Fielding cannot venture abroad without getting into trouble."

"And getting out of it, I thank you," rejoined Helen, somewhat offended by Mercy's remark.

"Certainly I have not been killed yet," was Ruth's mild observation, pinching Helen's arm to warn her that she was not to quarrel with the rather caustic lame girl. Mercy's affliction, which still somewhat troubled her, had never improved her naturally crabbed disposition, and few of her girl friends had Ruth's patience with her.

"I don't know that I feel much like seeing cowboys rope steers and all that after seeing that horrid black bull charge our Ruthie," complained Helen. "Shall we really go to the show?"

"Why! Ruth just told that girl we would," said Jennie.

"I wouldn't miss seeing that Wonota shoot for anything," Ruth declared.

"But there is nobody here to watch the automobile now," went on Helen, who was more nervous than her chum.

"Yes," Jennie remarked. "Here comes 'Silas Simpkins, the straw-chewing rube,'" and she giggled.

The farmer was at hand, puffing and blowing. He assured them that "that critter" was tightly housed and would do no more harm.

"Hope none o' you warn't hurt," he added. "By jinks! that bull is jest as much excited by this here Wild West Show as I be. Did you pay me for your ortymobile, young ladies?"

"I most certainly did," said Ruth. "Your bull did not drive all memory away."

"All right. All right," said the farmer hastily. "I thought you did, but I wasn't positive you'd remember it."

With which frank confession he turned away to meet another motor-car party that was attempting to park their machine on his land.

The four girls got out into the dusty road and marched to the ticket wagon that was gaily painted with the sign of "Dakota Joe's Wild West and Frontier Round-Up."

"This is my treat," declared Ruth, going ahead to the ticket window with the crowd. "I certainly should pay for all this excitement I have got you girls into."

Alice B. Emerson

"Go as far as you like," said Jennie. "But to tell the truth, I think the owner of the black bull should be taxed for this treat."

Dakota Joe's show was apparently very popular, for people were coming to it not only from Longhaven and Cheslow, but from many other towns and hamlets. This afternoon performance attracted many women and children, and when the four young women from Cheslow got into their reserved seats they found that they were right in the midst of a lot of little folks.

The big ring, separated from the plank seats by a board fence put up in sections, offered a large enough tanbark-covered course to enable steers to be roped, bucking broncos exhibited, Indian riding races, and various other events dear to the heart of the Wild West Show fans. And the program of Dakota Joe's show was much like that of similar exhibitions. He had some "real cowboys" and "sure-enough Indians," as well as employees who were not thus advertised. The steers turned loose for the cowboys to "bulldog" were rather tame animals, for they were used to the employment. The "bronco busters" rode trick horses so well trained that they really acted better than their masters. Some of the roping and riding—especially by the Indians—was really good.

And then came a number on the program that the four girls from Cheslow had impatiently awaited. The announcer (Dakota Joe himself, on horseback and wearing hair to his shoulders *a la* Buffalo Bill) rode into the center of the ring and held up a gauntleted hand for attention.

"We now offer you, ladies and gentlemen, an exhibition in rifle shooting second to none on any program of any show in America to-day. The men of the old West were most wonderful shots with rifle or six-gun. To-day the new West produces a rifle shot that equals Wild Bill Hickok, Colonel

Cody himself, or Major Lillie. And to show that the new West, ladies and gentlemen, is right up to the minute in this as in every other pertic'lar, we offer Wonota, daughter of Chief Totantora, princess of the Osage Indians, in a rifle-shooting act that, ladies and gentlemen, is simply marv'lous—simply marv'lous!"

He waved a lordly hand, the band struck up a strident tune, and on a "perfect love of a white pony," as Helen declared, Wonota rode into the ring.

She looked just as calm as she had when she had shot the bull which threatened Ruth. Nothing seemed to flutter the Indian girl's pulse or to change her staid expression. Yet the girls noticed that Dakota Joe spurred his big horse to the white pony's side, and, unless they were mistaken, the man said something to Wonota in no pleasant manner.

"Look at that fellow!" exclaimed Helen. "Hasn't he an ugly look?"

"I guess he didn't say anything pleasant to her," Ruth rejoined, for she was a keen observer. "I shouldn't wonder if that girl was far from happy."

"I shouldn't want to work for that Dakota Joe," added Mercy Curtis. "Look at him!"

Unable to make Wonota's expression of countenance change, the man, who was evidently angry with the Indian girl, struck the white pony sharply with his whip. The pony jumped, and some of the spectators, thinking it a part of the program, laughed.

Unexpecting Dakota Joe's act, Wonota was not prepared for her mount's jump. She was almost thrown from the saddle. But the next instant she had tightened the pony's rein, hauled

Alice B. Emerson

it back on its haunches with a strong hand, and wheeled the animal to face Dakota Joe.

What she said to the man certainly Ruth and her friends could not understand. It was said in the Osage tongue in any case. But with the words the Indian girl thrust forward the light rifle which she carried. For a moment its blue muzzle was set full against the white man's chest.

"Oh!" gasped Jennie. And she was not alone in thus giving vent to her excitement. "Oh!"

"Why doesn't she shoot him?" drawled Mercy Curtis.

"I—I guess It was only in fun," said Helen rather shakingly, as the Indian girl wheeled her mount again and rode away from Dakota Joe.

"I wouldn't want her to be that funny with me," gasped Jennie Stone. "She must be a regular wild Indian, after all."

"I am sure, at least, that this Dakota Joe person would have deserved little sympathy if she had shot him," declared Mercy, with confidence.

"Dear me," admitted Ruth herself, "I want to meet that girl more than ever now. There must be some mystery regarding her connection with the owner of the show. They certainly are not in accord."

"You've said something!" agreed Jennie, likewise with conviction.

If Wonota had been at all flurried because of her treatment by her employer, she no longer showed it. Having ridden to the proper spot, she wheeled the white pony again and faced the place where there was a steel shield against which the objects she was to shoot at were thrown.

Dakota Joe rode forward as though to affix the first clay ball to the string. Then he pulled in his horse, scowled across the ring at Wonota, and beckoned one of the cowboys to approach. This man took up the duty of affixing the targets for the Indian girl.

"Do you see that?" chuckled Jennie Stone. "He's afraid she might change her mind and shoot him after all."

"Sh!" cautioned Ruth. "Somebody might hear you. Now look."

The swinging targets were shattered by Wonota as fast as the man could hook them to the string and set the string to swinging. Then he threw glass balls filled with feathers into the air for the Indian girl to explode.

It was evident that she was not doing as well as usual, for she missed several shots. But this was not because of her own nervousness. Since the pony had been cut with Dakota Joe's whip it would not stand still, and its nervousness was plainly the cause of Wonota's misses.

The owner of the show was, however, the last person to admit this. He showed more than annoyance as the act progressed.

Perhaps it was the strained relations so evident between the owner of the show and Wonota that affected the man attending to the targets, for he became rather wild. He threw a glass ball so far to one side that to have shot at it would have endangered the spectators, and the Indian girl dropped the muzzle of her rifle and shook her head. The curving ball came within Dakota Joe's reach.

Alice B. Emerson

"Some baseball player, I'll say!" ejaculated Jennie Stone slangily.

For the owner of the show caught the flying ball. He wheeled his spirited horse, and, holding the ball at arm's length, he spurred down the field toward the Indian girl.

"Oh!" cried Ruth under her breath. "He is going to throw it at her!"

"The villain!" ejaculated Mercy Curtis, her eyes flashing.

But if that was his intention, Dakota Joe did not fulfill it. The Indian girl whipped up the muzzle of her rifle and seemed to take deliberate aim at the angry man. Evidently this act was not on the bill!

CHAPTER IV

SMOKING THE PEACE PIPE

Ruth Fielding almost screamed aloud. She rose in her seat, clinging to Helen Cameron's arm.

"Oh! what will she do?" gasped the girl of the Red Mill, just as the rifle in the Indian sharp-shooter's hands spat its brief tongue of flame.

The glass ball in Dakota Joe's fingers was shattered and he went through a cloud of feathers as he turned his horse at a tangent and rode away from the Indian girl. It was a good shot, but one that the proprietor of the Wild West Show did not approve of!

"Oh!" exclaimed Mercy Curtis, bitterly, "why didn't she shoot him instead of the ball? He deserves it, I know."

"Dear me, Mercy," drawled Jennie Stone, "you most certainly are a blood-thirsty person!"

"I just know that man is a villain, and the Indian girl is in his power."

"Next reel!" giggled Helen. "It is a regular Western cinema drama, isn't it?"

28   Alice B. Emerson

"I certainly want to become better acquainted with that Wonota," declared Ruth, not at all sure but that Mercy Curtis was right in her opinion. "There! Wonota is going off."

The applause the Indian girl received was vociferous. Most of the spectators believed that the shooting of the glass ball out of the man's hand had been rehearsed and was one of Wonota's chief feats. Ruth and her friends had watched what had gone before too closely to make that mistake. There was plainly a serious schism between Dakota Joe and the girl whom he had called the Indian princess.

The girls settled back in their seats after Wonota had replied to the applause with a stiff little bow from the entrance to the dressing-tent. The usual representation of "Pioneer Days" was then put on, and while the "stage" was being set for the attack on the emigrant train and Indian massacre, the fellow who had stood at the pasture fence and talked to the girls when the black bull had done his turn, suddenly appeared in the aisle between the plank seats and gestured to Ruth.

"What?" asked the girl of the Red Mill "You want me?"

"You're the lady," he said, grinning. "Won't keep you a minute. You can git back and see the rest of the show all right."

"It must be that Wonota has sent him for me," explained Ruth, seeing no other possible reason for this call. Refusing to let even Helen go with her, she followed the man up the aisle and down a narrow flight of steps to the ground.

"What is the matter with her? What does she want me for?" Ruth asked him when she could get within earshot and away from the audience.

"Her?"

"Yes. You come from Wonota, don't you?"

The man chuckled, but still kept on. "You'll see her in a minute. Right this way, Miss," he said.

They came to a canvas-enclosed place with a flap pinned back as though it were the entrance to a tent. The guide flourished a hamlike hand, holding back the canvas flap.

"Just step in and you'll find her," he said, again chuckling.

Ruth was one not easily alarmed. But the fellow seemed impudent. She gave him a reproving look and marched into what appeared to be an office, for there was a desk and a chair in view.

There, to her surprise, was Dakota Joe, the long-haired proprietor of the Wild West Show! He stood leaning against a post, his arms folded and smoking a very long and very black cigar. He did not remove his hat as Ruth entered, but rolled his cigar from one corner of his mouth to the other and demanded harshly:

"You know this Injun girl I got with the show?"

"Certainly I know her!" Ruth exclaimed without hesitation, "She saved my life."

"Huh! I heard about that, ma'am. And I don't mean it just that way. I'm talking about her—drat her! She says she has got a date with you and your friends between the afternoon and night shows."

"Yes," Ruth said wonderingly. "We are to meet—and talk."

"That's just it, ma'am," said the man, rolling the cigar again in an offensive way. "That's just it. When you come to talk

Alice B. Emerson

with that Injun girl, I want you to steer her proper on one p'int. We're white, you an' me, and I reckon white folks will stick together when it comes to a game against reds. Get me?"

"I do not think I do—yet," answered Ruth hesitatingly.

"Why, see here, now," Dakota Joe went on. "It's easy to see you're a lady—a white lady. I'm a white gent. This Injun wench has got it in for me. Did you see what she come near doin' to me right out there in the ring?"

Ruth restrained a strong wish to tell him exactly what she had seen. But somehow she felt that caution in the handling of this rough man would be the wiser part.

"I saw that she made a very clever shot in breaking that ball in your hand, Mr. Dakota Joe," the girl of the Red Mill said.

"Heh? Well, didn't you see she aimed straight at me? Them reds ain't got no morals. They'd jest as lief shoot a feller they didn't like as not. We have to keep 'em down all the time. I know. I been handling 'em for years."

"Well, sir?" asked Ruth impatiently.

"Why, this Wonota—drat her!—is under contract with me. She's a drawin' card, I will say. But she's been writin' back to the agency where I got her and making me trouble. She means to leave me flat if she can—and a good winter season coming on."

"What do you expect me to do about it, Mr.—er—Dakota Joe?" asked Ruth.

"Fenbrook. Fenbrook's my name, ma'am," tardily explained the showman. "Now, see here. She's nothin' but an ignorant redskin. Yep. She's daughter of old Totantora, hereditary chief of the Osages. But he's out of the way and her guardian is the Indian Agent at Three Rivers Station in Oklahoma where the Osages have their reservation. As I say, this gal has writ to the agent and told him a pack o' lies about how bad she is treated. And she ain't treated bad a mite."

"Well, Mr. Fenbrook?" demanded Ruth again.

"Why, see now. This Injun gal thinks well of you. I know what she's told the other performers. And I see her looking at you. Naturally, being nothin' but a redskin, she'll look up to a white lady like you. You tell her she's mighty well off here, all things considered—will you? Just tell her how hard some gals of her age have to work, while all she does is to ride and shoot in a show. All them Injuns is crazy to be play-actors, you know. Even old Chief Totantora was till he got mixed up with them Germans when the war come on.

"Huh? You savvy my idee, Miss? Jest tell her she's better off with the show than she would be anywhere else. Will you? Do as I say, Miss, and I'll slip you a bunch of tickets for all your friends. We're showin' at Great Forks on Friday, at Perryville Saturday, and at Lymansburg fust of the week. You can take your friends in and have fust-class seats to all them places."

"Thank you very much, Mr. Fenbrook," said Ruth, having difficulty to keep from laughing. "But owing to other engagements I could not possibly accept your kind offer. However, I will speak to the girl and advise her to the best of my ability."

Which was exactly what Ruth did when, later, she and her friends were met by the Princess Wonota at the exit of the big tent. The girl of the Red Mill had had no opportunity to explain to Helen and Jennie and Mercy in full about her interview with Dakota Joe. But she was quite decided as to what she proposed to do.

"Let us go on to the automobile, girls," Ruth said, taking Wonota's hand. "We want to talk where nobody will overhear us."

It was Mercy, when they arrived at Helen's car, who put the first question to the Indian maid:

"Why didn't you shoot that man? I would have done so!"

"Oh, hush, Mercy!" ejaculated Jennie Stone. "She will think you are quite a savage."

Helen laughed gaily and helped Wonota into the tonneau.

"Come on!" she cried. "Let us smoke the peace-pipe and tell each other all our past lives."

But Ruth remained rather grave, looking steadily at the Indian girl. When they were seated, she said:

"If you care to confide in us, Wonota, perhaps we can advise you, or even help you. I know that you are unhappy and unkindly treated at this show. I owe you so much that I would be glad to feel that I had done something for you in return."

The grave face of the Indian girl broke into a slow smile. When she did smile, Ruth thought her very winsome indeed. Now that she had removed her headdress and wore her black hair in two glossy plaits over her shoulders, she was even more attractive.

"You are very kind," Wonota said. "But perhaps I should not trouble you with any of my difficulties."

"If you have troubles," interposed Jennie, "you've come to the right shop. We all have 'em and a few more won't hurt us a bit. We're just dying to know why that man treats you so mean."

"He wouldn't treat me that way!" put in Mercy vigorously.

"But you see I—I am quite alone," explained Wonota. "Since Father Totantora went away I have been without any kin and almost without friends in our nation."

"That is it," said Ruth. "Begin at the beginning. Tell us how the chief came to leave you, and how you got mixed up with this Dakota Joe. I have a very small opinion of that man," added the girl of the Red Mill, "and I do not think you should remain in his care."

Alice B. Emerson

CHAPTER V

INSPIRATION

It was on the verge of evening, and a keen and searching wind was blowing across the ruffled Lumano, when Helen Cameron's car and its three occupants came in sight of the old Red Mill. Mercy Curtis had been dropped at the Cheslow railway station, where she had the "second trick" as telegraph operator.

For the last few miles of the journey from the Wild West Show there had been a good-natured, wordy battle between Ruth and Helen as to which of the twain was to have Jennie Stone for the night.

"Her trunk is at my house," Helen declared. "So now!"

"But her toilet bag is at the farmhouse. And, anyway, I could easily lend her pajamas."

"She could never get into a suit of yours, you know very well, Ruth Fielding!" exclaimed Helen.

"I'd get one of Uncle Jabez's long flannel nightgowns for her, then," giggled Ruth.

"Look here! I don't seem to be in such great favor with either of you, after all," interposed the plump girl. "One would think I was a freak. And I prefer my own night apparel in any case."

"Then you'll come home with me," Helen announced.

"But I have things at Ruth's house, just as she says," said Jennie.

At the moment the car wheeled around the turn in the road and Helen stopped it at the gate before the old, shingled farmhouse which was connected by a passage with the grist mill. A light flashed in the window and at once the place looked very inviting. A door opened upon the side porch, and to the girls' nostrils was wafted a most delicious odor of frying cakes.

"That settles it!" ejaculated Jennie Stone, and immediately sprang out of the car. "I'm as hungry as a bear. I'll see you to-morrow, Nell, if you'll ride over. But don't come too near mealtime. I never could withstand Aunt Alvirah's cooking. M-mm! Griddle-cakes—with lashin's of butter and sugar on 'em, I wager."

"Dear me!" sighed Helen, as Ruth, too, got out, laughing. "You are incurable, Jennie. Your goddess is your tummy."

But the plump girl was not at all abashed. She ran up the walk on to the porch and warmly greeted the little old woman who stood in the doorway.

"How-do, Jennie. Oh, my back and oh, my bones! Be careful, child! I'm kinder tottery to-day, and no mistake. Coming in, Helen Cameron?"

"Not to-night, Aunt Alvirah," replied the girl, starting the car again. "Good-night, all."

Alice B. Emerson

"And here's my pretty!" crooned Aunt Alvirah, putting up her thin arms to encircle Ruth's neck as the girl came in. "It does seem good to have you home again. Your Uncle Jabez (who is softer-hearted than you would suppose) is just as glad to have you home as I am, to be sure."

They had a merry supper in the wide, home-like kitchen, for even the miller when he came in was cheerful. He had had a good day at the grist mill. The cash-box was heavy that night, but he did not retire to his room to count his receipts as early as usual. The chatter of the two girls kept the old man interested.

"It is a shame that the Indian agent should let a girl like Wonota sign a contract with that Dakota Joe. Anybody might see, to look at him, that he was a bad man," Jennie Stone said with vehemence at one point in the discussion.

"I am not much troubled over that point for the girl," said Ruth. "She says she has already written to the agent at the Three Rivers Station, Oklahoma, telling him how badly Fenbrook treats her. That will soon be over. She will get her release."

"I shouldn't wonder," said Uncle Jabez, "that if a gal can fire a gun like you say she can, there ain't much reason to worry about her. She can take care of herself with that showman."

"But suppose she should be tempted to do something really desperate!" cried Ruth. "I hope nothing like that will happen. She is really a savage by instinct."

"And a pretty one," agreed Jennie, thoughtfully.

"Shucks! Pretty is as pretty does," said Aunt Alvirah. "I didn't s'pose there was any real wild Injuns left."

"You'd think she was wild," chuckled Jennie, "if you'd seen her draw bead on that Dakota Joe person."

"All that is not so much to the point," pursued Ruth. "I know that the girl wants to earn money—not alone for her mere living. She could go back to the reservation and live very comfortably without working—much. The Osage Nation is not at all poverty stricken and it holds its property ill community fashion."

"What makes her travel around in such a foolish way, then?" Aunt Alvirah asked.

"She wants ready cash. She wants it for a good purpose, too," explained Ruth thoughtfully. "You see, this girl's father is Chief Totantora, a leading figure in the Osage Nation. The year before Germany began the war he was traveling with a Wild West Show in Europe. The show was in the interior of Germany when war came and the frontiers were closed.

"Once only did Wonota hear from her father. He was then in a detention camp, for, being a good American, he refused to bow down to Hun gods—"

"I should say he had a right to call himself an American, if anybody has," said Jennie quickly.

"And he is not the only Indian who proved his loyalty to a Government that, perhaps, has not always treated the original Americans justly," Ruth remarked.

"I dunno," grumbled Uncle Jabez. "Injuns is Injuns. You say yourself this gal is pretty wild."

"She is independent, at any rate. She wishes to earn enough money to set afoot a private inquiry for Chief Totantora. For she does not believe he is dead."

"Well, the poor dear," Aunt Alvirah said, "she'd ought to be helped, I haven't a doubt."

"Now, now!" exclaimed the miller, suspiciously. "Charity begins at home. I hope you ain't figgerin' on any foolish waste of money, Niece Ruth."

The latter laughed. "I don't think Wonota would accept charity," she said. "And I have no intention of offering it to her in any case. But I should like to help the girl find her father—indeed I should."

"You'd oughtn't to think you have to help everybody you come 'cross in the world, gal," advised Uncle Jabez, finally picking up the cash-box to retire to his room. "Every tub ought to stand on its own bottom, as I've allus told ye."

When he was gone Aunt Alvirah shook her head sadly.

"Ain't much brotherhood of man in Jabez Potter's idees of life," she said. "He says nobody ever helped him get up in the world, so why should he help others?"

"Of all things!" exclaimed Ruth, with some warmth. "I wonder what he would have done all these years without you to make a home for him here!"

"Tut, tut!" objected the old woman. "'Tain't me that's done for him. I was a poor lone creeter in the poorhouse when Jabez Potter came and took me out. I know that deep down in his old heart there's a flame of charity. Who should know it better?"

"Oh, dear!" cried Ruth. "He keeps it wonderfully well hidden—that flame. He certainly does."

Jennie laughed. "Well, why shouldn't he be cautious? See

how many times you have been charitable, Ruth, and seen no gratitude in return."

"Well!" gasped the girl of the Red Mill, in disgust, "is *that* what we are to be charitable for? For shame!"

"Right you are, my pretty," said Aunt Alvirah. "Doin' one's duty for duty's sake is the way the good Lord intended. And if Jabez Potter is charitable without knowin' it—and he *is*— all the better. It's charged up to his credit in heaven, I have no doubt."

The girls were tired after their long ride in the keen evening air and they were ready for bed at a comparatively early hour. But after Ruth had got into bed she could not sleep.

Thoughts rioted in her brain. For a week she had felt the inspiration of creative work milling in her mind—that is what she called it. She had promised the president of the Alectrion Film Corporation to think up some unusual story— preferably an outdoor plot—for their next picture. And thus far nothing had formed in her mind that suggested the thing desired.

Outdoor stories had the call on the screen. They had but lately made one on the coast of Maine, the details of which are given in "Ruth Fielding Down East." Earlier in her career as a screen writer the girl of the Red Mill had made a success of a subject which was photographed in the mining country of the West. "Ruth Fielding in the Saddle" tells the story of this venture.

There spun through her half-drowsing brain scenes of the Wild West Show they had attended this day. That was surely "outdoor stuff." Was there anything in what she had seen to-day to suggest a novel scheme for a moving picture?

Alice B. Emerson

She turned and tossed. Her eyes would not remain closed. The program of Dakota Joe's Wild West and Frontier Round-Up marched in sequence through her memory. She did not want anything like that in her picture. It was all "old stuff," and the crying need of the film producer is "something new under the sun."

Yet there was color and action in much of the afternoon's performance. Even Dakota Joe himself—as the figure of a villain, for instance—was not to be scorned. And Princess Wonota herself—

If the story was up to date, showing the modern, full-blooded Indian princess in love and action! Ruth suddenly bounded out of bed. She grabbed a warm robe, wrapped herself in it and ran across to Jennie's room.

"Jennie! Jennie! I've got it!" Ruth cried in a loud whisper.

Jennie's only answer was a prolonged and pronounced snore! She was lying on her back.

"Jennie Stone!" exclaimed Ruth, shaking the plump girl by the shoulder.

"Wo—wow—ough! Is it fire?" gasped Jennie, finally aroused.

"No, no! I've got it!" repeated Ruth.

"Well—ell—I hope it isn't catching," said the other rather crossly. "You've spoiled—ow!—my beauty sleep, Ruthie Fielding."

"Listen!" commanded her friend. "I've the greatest idea for a picture. I know Mr. Hammond will be delighted. I am going to get Wonota on contract when she breaks with Dakota Joe.

I'll make her the central figure of a big picture. She shall be the leading lady."

"Why, Ruthie Fielding! that's something you have never yet done for me, and I have been your friend for years and years."

"Never mind. When it seems that the time is ripe to screen a story about a pretty, plump girl, you shall have an important part in the production," promised Ruth. "But listen to me—do! I am going to make Princess Wonota an Indian star—"

"I believe you," drawled the plump girl. "I suppose you might call her a 'shooting star'?"

Alice B. Emerson

CHAPTER VI

EVERYBODY AGREES BUT DAKOTA JOE

An inspiration is all right—even when it strikes one in the middle of the night. So Jennie Stone remarked. But there had to be something practical behind such a venture as Ruth Fielding had suggested to the sleepy girl.

Her thought regarding Princess Wonota of the Osage Tribe was partly due to her wish to help the Indian girl, and partly due to her desire to furnish Mr. Hammond and the Alectrion Film Corporation with another big feature picture.

Ruth and Jennie (who became enthusiastic when she was awake in the morning) chattered about the idea like magpies from breakfast to lunch. Then Helen drove over from The Outlook, and she had to hear it all explained while Ruth and Jennie were making ready to go out in the car with her.

"You must drive us right to Cheslow," Ruth said, "where I can get Mr. Hammond on the long-distance 'phone. This is important. I feel that I have a really good idea."

"But what do you suppose that Dakota Joe will say?" drawled Helen. "He won't love you, I fear."

"Has he got to know?" demanded Jennie. "Don't be a goose,

Helen. This is all going to be done on the q.t."

"Very well," sniffed the other girl. "Guess you'll find it difficult to take Wonota away from the Wild West Show without Joe's knowing anything about it."

"Of course!" laughed Ruth. "But until the fatal break occurs we must not let him suspect anything."

"I see. It is a fell conspiracy," remarked Helen. "Well, come on! The chariot awaits, my lady. If I am to drive a bunch of conspirators, let's be at it."

"Helen would hustle one around," complained Jennie, "if she were in the plot to kill Caesar."

"Your tense is bad, little lady," said Helen. "Caesar, according to the books, has been dead some years now. Right-o?"

The girls sped away from the old mill, and in a little while Ruth was shut into a telephone booth talking with Mr. Hammond in a distant city. She told him a good deal more than she had the girls. It was his due. Besides, she had already got the skeleton of a story in her mind and she repeated the important points of this to the picture producer.

"Sounds good, Miss Ruth," he declared. "But it all depends upon the girl. If you think she has the looks, is amenable to discipline, and has some natural ability, we might safely go ahead with it, I will get into communication by telegraph with the Department of Indian Affairs at Washington and with the agent at Three Rivers Station, Oklahoma, as well. We can afford to invest some money in the chance that this Wonota is a find."

"Fifty-fifty, Mr. Hammond," Ruth told him. "On whatever it

costs, remember, I am just as good a sport as you are when it comes to taking a chance in business."

He laughed. "I have often doubted your blood relationship to Uncle Jabez," Mr. Hammond declared "He has no gambler's blood in his old veins."

"He was born too long before the moving picture came into existence," she laughingly returned. "Now I mean to see Wonota again and try to encourage her to throw in her fortunes with us. At least, I hope to get her away from that disgusting Dakota Joe."

Later Jennie teasingly suggested: "You should have taken up with his offer, Ruthie. You could have had free passes to the show in several towns."

"I don't much wish to see the show again," Ruth declared.

"I bet Mercy Curtis would like to see it," giggled Helen, "if Wonota was sure to shoot Joe. What a bloodthirsty child that Mercy continues to be."

"She has changed a lot since we were all children together," Ruth said reflectively. "And I never did blame Mercy much for being so scrappy. Because of her lameness she missed a lot that we other girls had. I am so glad she has practically gotten over her affliction."

"But not her failings of temper," suggested Jennie. "Still, as long as she takes it out on Dakota Joe, for instance, I don't know but I agree with her expressions of savage feeling."

"Hear! Hear!" cried Helen.

Despite their expressed dislike for Fenbrook, Helen and Jennie Stone accompanied Ruth the next day to the afternoon performance of the Wild West Show at a town much farther away than that at which they had first met Wonota, the Indian princess.

Wonota was glad to see them—especially glad to see Ruth Fielding. For Ruth had given her hope for a change. The Indian girl was utterly disillusioned about traveling with a tent show; and even the promises Fenbrook had made her of improved conditions during the winter, when they would show for week-runs in the bigger cities, did not encourage Wonota to continue with him.

"Yet I would very much like to earn money to spend in searching for the great Chief Totantora," she confessed to the three white girls. "The Great Father at Washington can do nothing now to find my father—and I do not blame the White Father. The whole world is at war and those peoples in Europe are sick with the fever of war. It is sad, but it cannot be helped."

"And if you had money how would you go about looking for Chief Totantora?" Helen asked her curiously.

"I must go over there myself. I must search through that German country."

"Plucky girl!" ejaculated Jennie. "But not a chance!"

"You think not, lady?" asked Wonota, anxiously.

"We three have been to Europe—to France. We know something about the difficulties," said Ruth, quietly. "I understand how you feel, Wonota. And conditions may soon change. We believe the war will end. Then you can make a proper search for your father."

"But not unless I have much money," said Wonota quickly.

Alice B. Emerson

"The Osage people have valuable oil lands on their reservation. But it will be some years before money from them will be available, so the agent tells me. That is why I came with this show."

"And that is why you wish to keep on earning money?" suggested Ruth reflectively.

"That is why," Wonota returned, nodding.

At this point in the conversation the showman himself came up. He smirked in an oily manner at the white girls and tried to act kindly toward his pretty employee. Wonota scarcely looked in the man's direction, but Ruth of course was polite in her treatment of Dakota Joe.

"I see you're doin' like I asked you, ma'am," he hoarsely whispered behind his hairy hand to the girl of the Red Mill. "What's the prospect?"

"I could scarcely tell you yet, Mr. Fenbrook," Ruth said decidedly. "Wonota must decide for herself, of course."

"Humph! Wal, if she knows what's best for her she'll aim to stay right with old Dakota Joe. I'm her best friend."

Ruth left the girl at this time with some encouraging words. She had told her that if she, Wonota, could get a release from her contract with the showman there would be an opportunity for her to earn much more money, and under better conditions, in the moving picture business.

"Oh!" cried Wonota with sparkling eyes, "do you think I could act for the movies? I have often wanted to try."

"There it is," said Helen, as the girls drove home. "Even the Red Indian is crazy to act in the movies. Can you beat it?"

"Well," Ruth asked soberly, "who is there that is not interested in getting his or her picture taken? Not very many. And when it comes to appearing on the silver sheet—well, even kings and potentates fall for that!"

Ruth was so sure that Wonota could be got into the moving pictures and that Mr. Hammond would be successful in making a star of the Indian girl, that that very night she sat up until the wee small hours laying out the plot of her picture story—the story which she hoped to make into a really inspirational film.

There was coming, however, an unexpected obstacle to this achievement—an obstacle which at first seemed to threaten utter failure to her own and to Mr. Hammond's plans.

Alice B. Emerson

CHAPTER VII

DAKOTA JOE'S WRATH

It was a crisp day with that tang of frost in the air that makes the old shiver and the young feel a tingling in the blood. Aunt Alvirah drew her chair closer to the stove in the sitting-room. She had a capable housework helper now, and even Jabez Potter made no audible objection, for Ruth paid the bill, and the dear old woman had time to sit and talk to "her pretty" as she loved to do.

"Oh, my back and oh, my bones!" she murmured, as she settled into her rocking-chair. "I am a leetle afraid, my pretty, that you will have your hands full if you write pictures for red savages to act. It does seem to me they air dangerous folks to have anything to do with.

"Why, when I was a mite of a girl, I heard my great-grandmother tell that when she was a girl she went with her folks clean acrosst the continent—or, leastways, beyond the Mississippi, and they drove in a big wagon drawed by oxen."

"Goodness! They went in an emigrant train?" cried Ruth.

"Not at all. 'Twarn't no train," objected Aunt Alvirah. "Trains warn't heard of then. Why, *I* can remember when the first railroad went through this part of the country and it cut right through Silas Bassett's farm. They told him he could go down to the tracks any time he felt like going to town, wave his hat, and the train would stop for him."

"Well, wasn't that handy?" cried the girl.

"It sounded good. But Silas didn't have it on paper. First off they did stop for him if he hailed the train. He didn't go to town more'n three or four times a year. Then the railroad changed hands. 'There arose up a new king over Egypt which knew not Joseph'—you know, like it says in the Bible. And when Silas Bassett waved his hat, the train didn't even hesitate!"

Ruth laughed, but reminded her that they were talking about her great-grandmother's adventures in the Indian country years and years before.

"Yes, that's a fact," said Aunt Alvirah Boggs. "She did have exciting times. Why, when they was traveling acrosst them Western prairies one day, what should pop up but a band of Indians, with tall feathers in their hair, and guns—mebbe bow and arrows, too. Anyway, they scare't the white people something tremendous," and the old woman nodded vigorously.

"Well, the neighbors who were traveling together hastened to turn their wagons so as to make a fortress sort of, of the wagon-bodies, with the horses and the cattle and the humans in the center. You understand?"

"Yes," Ruth agreed. "I have seen pictures of such a camp, with the Indians attacking."

"Yes. Well, but you see," cackled the old woman suddenly, "them, Indians didn't attack at all. They rode down at a gallop, I expect, and scared the white folks a lot But what they come for was to see if there was a doctor in the party. Those Indians had heard of white doctors and knowed what they could do. The chief of the tribe had a favorite child that was very sick, and he come to see if a white doctor could save his child's life."

"Oh!" cried Ruth, her eyes sparkling. "What an idea!"

"Well, my pretty, I dunno," said Aunt Alvirah. "'Twas sensible enough, I should say, for that Indian chief to want the best doctoring there was for his child. The medicine men had tried to cure the poor little thing and failed. I expect even Red Indians sometimes love their children."

"Why, of course, Aunt Alvirah. And you ought to see how lovable this girl Wonota is."

"Mm—well, mebbe. Anyway, there was a doctor in that party my great-grandmother traveled with, and he rode to the Indian village and cured the sick child. And for the rest of their journey across them plains Indians, first of one tribe, then of another, rode with the party of whites. And they never had no trouble."

"Isn't that great!" cried Ruth.

And when she told Helen and Jennie about it—and the idea it had given Ruth for a screen story—her two chums agreed that it was "perfectly great."

So Ruth was hard at work on a scenario, or detailed plot, even before Mr. Hammond made his arrangements with the Indian Department for the transferring of the services of Princess Wonota from Dakota Joe's Wild West Show to the Alectrion Film Corporation for a certain number of months.

The matter had now gone so far that it could not be kept

from Dakota Joe. He had spent money and pulled all the wires he could at the reservation to keep "Dead-Shot" Wonota in his employ. At first he did not realize that any outside agency was at work against him and for die girl's benefit.

Ruth and her friends drove to a distant town to see the Indian girl when the Wild West Show played for two days. They attended the matinee and saw Wonota between the two performances and had dinner with her at the local hotel. After dinner they all went to an attorney's office, where the papers in the case were ready, and Wonota signed her new contract and Helen and Jennie were two of the witnesses thereto. Mr. Hammond could not be present, but he had trusted to Ruth's good sense and business acumen.

In a week—giving Dakota Joe due notice—the old contract would be dead and Wonota would be at liberty under permission from the Indian Agent to leave the show. As Helen stopped the car before the torch-lighted entrance to the show for Wonota to step out, Dakota Joe strode out to the side of the road. He was scowling viciously.

"What's the matter with you, Wonota?" he demanded. "You trying to queer the show? You ain't got no more'n enough time to dress for your act. Get on in there, like I tell you."

Instead of propitiating Ruth now, he showed her the ugly side of his character.

"I guess you been playin' two-faced, ain't you, ma'am?" he growled as Wonota fled toward the dressing tent "I thought you was a friend of mine. But I believe you been cuttin' the sand right out from under my feet. Ain't you?"

"I do not know what you mean, Mr. Fenbrook," said Ruth sharply.

Alice B. Emerson

"You're Ruth Fielding, ain't you?" he demanded.

"Yes. That is my name."

"So they tell me," growled Dakota Joe. "And you are coupled up with this Hammond feller that they tell me has put in a bid for Wonota over and above what she's wuth, and what I can pay. Ain't that so?"

"If you wish to discuss the matter with Mr. Hammond I will give you his address," Ruth said with dignity. "I am not prepared to discuss the matter with you, Mr. Fenbrook."

"Is that so?" he snarled. "Well, ma'am, whether you want to talk or don't want to talk, things ain't goin' all your way. No, ma'am! I got some rights. The courts will give me my rights to Wonota. I'm her guardian, I am. Her father, Totantora, is dead, and I'll show you folks—and that Injun agent—just where you get off in this business!"

"Go on," said Ruth to Helen, without answering the angry man. But when the car had gone a little way along the road, the girl of the Red Mill exclaimed:

"Dear me! I fear that man will make trouble. I—I wish Tom were here."

"Don't say a word!" gasped Helen. "But not only because he could handle this Western bully do I wish Tommy-boy was home and the war was over."

"Why don't you offer Dakota Joe a job in your picture company, too?" drawled Jennie Stone.

"He'd make such a fine 'bad man.'"

"He certainly would," agreed Helen.

Just how bad the proprietor of the Wild West Show could be was proved the following day. Mr. Hammond sent Ruth a telegram In the morning intimating that something had gone wrong with their plans to get Wonota into their employ.

* * * * *

"The Court has given Fenbrook an injunction. What do you know about it?"

* * * * *

Now, of course, Ruth Fielding did not know anything at all about it. And after what she had seen of Dakota Joe she had no mind to go to him on behalf of Mr. Hammond and herself. If the Westerner was balking the attempt to get Wonota out of his clutches, nothing would beat him, Ruth believed, but legal proceedings.

She telegraphed Mr. Hammond to this effect, advising that he put the matter in the hands of the attorney that had drawn the new contract with the Indian girl.

"The goodness knows," she told Aunt Alvirah and Uncle Jabez, "I don't want to have anything personally to do with that rough man. He is just as ugly as he can be."

"Wal," snorted the miller, "he better not come around here cutting up his didoes! Me and Ben will tend to him!"

Ruth could not help being somewhat fearful of the proprietor of the Wild West Show. If the man really made up his mind to make trouble, Ruth hoped that he would not come to the Red Mill.

Helen and Jennie drove over to the mill to get Ruth that afternoon, and they planned to take Aunt Alvirah out with

Alice B. Emerson

them. She had lost her fear of the automobile and had even begun to hint to the miller that she wished he would buy a small car.

"Land o' Goshen!" grumbled Uncle Jabez, "what next? I s'pose you'd want to learn to run the dratted thing, Alvirah Boggs?"

"Well, Jabez Potter, I don't see why not?" she had confessed. "Other women learns."

"Huh! You with one foot in the grave and the other on the gas, eh?" he snorted.

However, Aunt Alvirah did not go out in Helen's car on this afternoon. While the girls were waiting for her to be made ready, Helen looked back, up the road, down which she and Jennie had just come.

"What's this?" she wanted to know. "A runaway horse?"

Jennie stood up to look over the back of the car. She uttered an excited squeal.

"Helen! Ruthie!" she declared. "It's that Indian girl—in all her war-togs, too. She is riding like the wind. And, yes! There is somebody after her! Talk about your moving picture chases—this is the real thing!"

"It's Dakota Joe!" shrieked Helen. "Goodness! He must have gone mad. See him beating that horse he rides. Why—"

"He surely has blown up," stated Jennie Stone with conviction. "Ruthie! what are you going to do?"

CHAPTER VIII

A WONDERFUL EVENT

Wonota was a long way ahead of the Westerner. She was light and she bestrode a horse with much more speed than the one Dakota Joe rode. She lay far along her horse's neck and urged it with her voice rather than a cruel goad.

The plucky pony was responding nobly, although it was plain, as it came nearer to the girls before the old mill farmhouse, that it had traveled hard. It was thirty miles from the town where the Wild West Show was performing to the Red Mill.

"Oh, Wonota!" cried Jennie Stone, beckoning the Indian girl on. "What is the matter?"

Ruth had not waited to get any report from Wonota. She turned and dashed for the house. Already Sarah, the maid-of-all-work, had started through the covered passage to the mill, shrieking for Ben, the hired man.

Ben and the miller ran down the long walk to roadside. Jabez Potter was no weakling despite his age, while Ben was a giant of a fellow, able to handle two ordinary men.

Wonota pulled her pony in behind Helen's car, whirling to

Alice B. Emerson

face her pursuer. She did not carry the light rifle she used in her act. Perhaps it would have been better had she been armed, for Dakota Joe was quite beside himself with wrath. He came pounding along, swinging his whip and yelling at the top of his voice.

"What's the matter with that crazy feller?" demanded the old miller in amazement. "He chasin' that colored girl?"

"She's not colored. She is my Indian princess, Uncle Jabez," Ruth explained.

"I swanny, you don't mean it! Hi, Ben!" But nobody had to tell Ben what to do. As Fenbrook drew in his horse abruptly, the mill-hand jumped into the road, grabbed Dakota Joe's whip-hand, broke his hold on the reins, and dragged the Westerner out of the saddle. It was a feat requiring no little strength, and it surprised Dakota Joe as much as it did anybody.

"Hey, you! What you doin'?" bawled Dakota Joe, when he found himself sitting on the hard ground, staring up at the group.

"Ain't doing nothing," drawled Ben. "It's done. Better sit where you be, Mister, and cool off."

"What sort o' tomfoolishness is this?" asked the miller again. "Makin' one o' them picture-shows right here on the public road? I want to know!"

At that, and without rising from his seat in the road, Dakota Joe Fenbrook lifted up his voice and gave his opinion of all moving picture people, and especially those that would steal "that Injun gal" from a hard-working man like himself. He stated that the efforts of a "shark named Hammond" and this girl here that he thought was a lady an' friendly to him were about to ruin his show.

"They'll crab the whole business if they git Wonota away from me. That's what will happen! And I ought to give her a blame' good lickin'—"

"We won't hear nothing more about that," interrupted the old miller, advancing a stride or two toward the angry Westerner. "Whether the gal's got blue blood or red blood, or what color, she ain't going to be mishandled none by you. Understand? You git up and git!"

"But what has happened, Wonota?" the puzzled Ruth asked the Indian girl.

Wonota pointed scornfully at Fenbrook, just then struggling to his feet.

"Joe, heap smart white man. Wuh!" She really was grimly chuckling. "He go get a talking paper from the court. Call it injunction, eh?"

"I heard about the injunction," admitted Ruth interestedly.

"All right Wonota can't leave Joe to work for you, eh? But the paleface law-man say to me that that talking paper good only In that county. You see? I not in that county now."

"Oh, Jerry!" gasped Jennie Stone. "Isn't that cute? She is outside the jurisdiction of the court."

"Sho!" exclaimed Jabez Potter, much amused by this outcome of the matter. "It is a fact. Go on back to your show, mister. The gal's here, and she's with friends, and that's all there is to it."

Dakota Joe had already realized this situation. He climbed

Alice B. Emerson

slowly into his saddle and eyed them all—especially Ruth and Wonota—with a savage glare.

"Wait!" he growled. "Wait—that's all. I'll fix you movie people yet—the whole of you! It's the sorriest day's job you ever done to get Wonota away from me. Wait!"

He rode away. When he was some rods up the road, down which he had galloped, he set spurs to his horse again and dashed on and out of sight. For a little while nobody spoke. It was Jennie who, as usual, light-hearted and unafraid, broke the silence.

"Well, all right, we'll wait," she said. "But we needn't do it right here, I suppose. We can sit down and wait just as easily."

Helen laughed. But Ruth and Wonota were sober, and even Uncle Jabez Potter saw something to take note of in the threat of the proprietor of the Wild West Show.

"That man is a coward. That's as plain as the nose on your face. And a coward when he gits mad and threatens you is more to be feared than a really brave man. That man's a coward. He's mean. He's p'ison mean! You want to look out for him, Niece Ruth. I wouldn't wonder if he tried, some time, to do you and Mr. Hammond some trick that won't bring you in no money, to say the least."

The old miller went off with that statement on his lips. Ben, the hired man, followed him, shaking his head. The girls looked at each other, then at the rapidly disappearing cloud of dust raised by Dakota Joe's pony. Jennie said:

"Well, goodness! why so serious? Guess that man won't do such a much! Don't be scared, Wonota. We won't let anybody hurt you."

"I wish Tom were here," Ruth Fielding repeated.

And in less than forty-eight hours this wish of the girl of the Red Mill seemed to her almost prophetical. Tom Cameron was coming home!

The whole land rejoiced over that fact. The whole world, indeed, gave thanks that it was possible for a young captain in the American Expeditionary Forces to look forward to his release and return to his home.

The armistice had been declared. Cheslow, like every town and city in the Union, celebrated the great occasion. It was not merely a day's celebration. The war was over (or so it seemed) and the boys who were so much missed would be coming home again. It took some time for Ruth and her friends to realize that this return must be, because of the nature of things, postponed for many tiresome months.

Before Tom Cameron was likely to be freed from the army, the matter of the Indian girl's engagement with the moving picture corporation must be completely settled—at least, as far as Dakota Joe's claim upon Wonota's services went.

Alice B. Emerson

CHAPTER IX

THE PLOT DEVELOPS

Ruth had insisted upon Wonota's remaining at the Red Mill from the hour she had ridden there for protection. Not that they believed Fenbrook would actually harm the Indian girl after he had cooled down. But it was better that she should be in Ruth's care as long as she was to work somewhat under the latter's tutelage.

Besides, it gave the picture writer a chance to study her subject. It would be too much to expect that Wonota could play a difficult part. She had had no experience in acting. Ruth knew that she must fit a part to Wonota, not the girl to a part. In other words, the Indian girl was merely a type for screen exploitation, and the picture Ruth wrote must be fitted to her capabilities.

Grasping, like any talented writer does, at any straw of novelty, Ruth had seen possibilities in the little incident Aunt Alvirah had told about her ancestor who had crossed the Western plains in the early emigrant days. She meant to open her story with a similar incident, as a prologue to the actual play.

Ruth made her heroine (the part she wished to fit to Wonota, the Osage Indian girl) repay in part the debt her family owed the white physician by saving a descendant of the physician from peril in the Indian country. This young man, the hero, is attracted by the Indian maid who has saved his life; but he is under the influence of a New York girl, one of the tourist party, to whom he is tentatively engaged.

But the New York girl deserts the hero when he gets into difficulty in New York. He is accused of a crime that may send him to the penitentiary for a long term and there seems no way to disprove the crime. Word of his peril comes to the Indian maid in her Western home. She knows and suspects the honesty of the timber men with whom the hero is connected in business. She discovers these villains are the guilty ones, and she travels to New York to testify for him and to clear him of the charge. The end of the story, as well as the beginning, was to be filmed in the wilds.

With the incidents of her plot gradually taking form in her mind and being jotted down on paper, Ruth's hours began to be very full. She was with Wonota as much as possible, and the Indian girl began to show an almost doglike devotion to the girl of the Red Mill.

"That is not to be wondered at, of course," Jennie Stone said, as she was about to return to her New York home. "Everybody falls for our Ruth. It's a wonder to me that she has not been elected to the presidency."

"Wait till we women get the vote," declared Helen. "Then we'll send Ruth to the chair."

"Goodness!" ejaculated Jennie. "That sounds terrible, Nell! One might think you mean the electric chair."

"Is there much difference, after all, between that and the presidential chair?" Helen demanded, chuckling. "The way some people talk about a president!"

"We are a loose-talking people," Ruth interrupted gravely, "and I think you girls talk almost as irresponsibly as anybody I ever heard."

"List to the stern and uncompromising Ruthie," scoffed Jennie. "I am glad I am going back to Aunt Kate. She is a spinster, I admit; but she isn't anywhere near as old-maid-like as Ruth Fielding."

"I'll tell Tom about that," said Tom's sister wickedly.

"Spinsters are the balance-wheel of the universe machinery," declared Ruth, laughing. "I always have admired them. But, joking aside, at this time when the whole world should be so grateful and so much in earnest because of the end of a terrible war, trivial matters and trivial talk somehow seems to jar."

"Not so! Not so!" cried Helen vigorously. "We have been holding in and trying to keep cheerful with the fear at our hearts that some loved one would suddenly be taken. It was not lightness of heart that made people dance and act as though rattled-pated during the war. It was an attempt to hide that awful fear in their hearts. See how the people in Cheslow acted as though they were crazy the night of the armistice. And did you read what the papers said about the times in New York? It was only a natural outbreak."

"Well," remarked. Ruth, shrugging her shoulders, "you certainly have got off the subject of old maids—bless 'em! Give my love to your Aunt Kate, Jennie, and when we come to the city to take the shots for this picture, I'll surely see her."

"Hi!" cried Miss Stone energetically. "I guess you will! You'll come right to the house and stay with us during that time!"

"Oh, no. I shall have Wonota with me. We will stay at a hotel. Our hours are always so uncertain when we shoot a picture that I could not undertake to be at any private house."

There was some discussion over this. Ruth did not intend to let Wonota out of her sight much while the picture was being made. Nor did she propose to let the script of the picture out of her sight until copies could be made of it, and the continuity man had made his version for the director. Ruth was not going to run the risk of losing another scenario, as she had once while Down East.

Ruth put in two weeks' hard work on the new story. As she laughingly said, she ate, slept, and talked movies all the time. Wonota had to amuse herself; but that did not seem hard for the Indian girl to do. She was naturally of a very quiet disposition. She sat by Aunt Alvirah for hours doing beadwork while the old woman darned or knitted.

"You wouldn't ever suspect she was a Red Indian unless you looked at her," Aunt Alvirah confessed to the rest of the family. "She's a very nice girl."

As for Wonota, she said:

"I used to sit beside my grandmother and work like this. Yes, Chief Totantora taught me to shoot and paddle a canoe, and to do many other things out-of-doors. But my grandmother was the head woman of our tribe, and her beadwork and dyed porcupine-quill work was the finest you ever saw, Ruth Fielding. I was sorry to leave my war-bag with Dakota Joe. It had in it many keepsakes my grandmother gave me before she passed to the Land of the Spirits."

A demand had been made upon the proprietor of the Wild West Show for Wonota's possessions, but the man had refused to give them up. The girl had not brought away with

Alice B. Emerson

her even the rifle she had used so successfully in the show. But her pony, West Wind, was stabled in the Red Mill barn. Indeed, Uncle Jabez had begun to hint that the animal was "eating its head off." The miller could not help showing what Aunt Alvirah called "his stingy streak" in spite of the fact that he truly was interested in the Indian maid and liked her.

"That redskin gal," he confessed in private to Ruth, "is a pretty shrewd and sensible gal. She got to telling me the other day how her folks ground grist in a stone pan, or the like, using a hard-wood club to pound it with. Right slow process of makin' flour or meal, I do allow.

"But what do you think she said when I put that up to her— about it's being a slow job?" and the miller chuckled. "Why, she told me that all her folks had was time, and they'd got to spend it somehow. They'd better be grinding corn by hand than making war on their neighbors or the whites, like they used to. She ain't so slow."

Ruth quite agreed with this. The Osage maiden was more than ordinarily intelligent, and she began to take a deep interest in the development of the story that Ruth was making for screen use.

"Am I to be that girl?" she asked doubtfully. "How can I play that I am in love when I have never seen a man I cared for— in that way?"

"Can't you imagine admiring a nice young man?" asked Ruth in return.

"Not a white man like this one in your story," Wonota said soberly. "It should be that he did more for himself—that he was more of a—a brave. We Indians do not expect our men to be saved from disgrace by women. Squaws are not counted of great value among the possessions of a chief."

"So you could not really respect such a man as I describe here if he allowed a girl to help him?" Ruth asked reflectively, for Wonota's criticism was giving her some thought.

"He should not be such a man—to need the help of a squaw," declared the Indian maid confidently. "But, of course, it does not matter if only palefaces are to see the picture."

But Ruth could not get the thought out of her mind. It might be that the Indian girl had suggested a real fault in the play she was making, and she took Mr. Hammond into her confidence about it when she sent him the first draft of the story. Her whole idea of the principal male character in "Brighteyes" might need recasting, and she awaited the picture producer's verdict with some misgiving.

While she waited a red-letter day occurred—so marked both for herself and for Helen Cameron. The chums had hoped— oh, how fondly!—that they would hear that Tom Cameron was on his way home. But gradually the fact that demobilization would take a long time was becoming a fixed idea in the girls' minds.

Letters came from Tom Cameron—one each for the two girls and one for Mr. Cameron. Instead of being on his way home, Captain Cameron had been sent even farther from the French port to which he had originally sailed in the huge transport from New York.

*   *   *   *   *

"I am now settled on the Rhine—one of the 'watches,' I suppose, that the Germans used to sing about, now stamped 'Made in America,' however," he wrote to Ruth. "We watch a bridge-head and see that the Germans don't carry away anything that might be needed on this side of the most

Alice B. Emerson

over-rated river in the world. I have come to the conclusion, since seeing a good bit of Europe, that most of the scenery is over-rated and does not begin to compare with the natural beauties of America. So many foreigners come to our shores and talk about the beauty-spots of their own countries, and so few Americans have in the past seen much of their own land, that we accept the opinions of homesick foreigners as to the superiority of the beauties of their father-and-mother-lands. After this war I guess there will be more fellows determined to give the States the 'once over.'"

*　*　*　*　*

Tom always wrote an interesting letter; but aside from that, of course Ruth was eager to hear from him. And now, as soon as she could, she sat down and replied to his communication. She had, too, a particular topic on which she wished to write her friend.

Now that embattled Germany would no longer hold its prisoners *incommunicado*, Ruth hoped that news about the imprisoned performers of the Wild West Show might percolate through the lines. Chief Totantora had been able but once to get a message to his daughter.

This message had reached America long before the United States had got into the war. Although the Osage chieftain was an American (who could claim such proud estate if Totantora could not?), the show by which he was employed had gone direct to Germany from England, and anything English had, from the first, been taboo in Germany. Now, of course, the Indian girl had no idea as to where her father was.

"See if you can hear anything about those performers," Ruth wrote to Tom. "Get word if you can to the Chief of the Osage Indians and tell him that his daughter is with me, and that she longs for his return.

"I should love to make her happy by aiding in Chief Totantora's reappearance in his native land. She is so sad, indeed, that I wonder if she is going to be able to register, for the screen, the happiness that she should finally show when my picture is brought to its conclusion."

Alice B. Emerson

CHAPTER X

ONE NEW YORK DAY

That "happy ending" became a matter of much thought on Ruth's part, and the cause of not a little argument between her and Mr. Hammond when he came up to Cheslow and the Red Mill to discuss "Brighteyes" with its youthful author. He had come, too, to get a glimpse of Wonota in the flesh.

One of the first things Ruth had done when the Indian girl came under her care was to take Wonota to Cheslow and have the best photographer of the town take several "stills" of the Indian girl. Copies of these she had sent to the Alectrion Film Corporation, and word had come back from both Mr. Hammond and his chief director that the photographs of Wonota were satisfactory.

The president of the film company, however, was interested in talking with Wonota and judging as far as possible through cursory examination just how much there was to the girl.

"What has she got in her? That is what we want to know," he said to Ruth. "Can she get expression into her face? Can she put over feeling? We want something besides mere looks, Miss Ruth, as you very well know."

"I realize all that," the girl of the Red Mill told him earnestly. "But remember, Mr. Hammond, you cannot judge this Osage girl by exactly the same standards as you would a white girl!"

"Why not? She's got to be able to show on the screen the deepest feelings of her nature—"

"Not if you would have my 'Brighteyes' true to life," interrupted Ruth anxiously. "You must not expect it."

"Why not?" he demanded again, with some asperity. "We don't want to show the people a dummy. I tell you the public is getting more and more critical. They won't stand for just pretty pictures. The actors In them must express their thoughts and feelings as they do in real life."

"Exactly!" Ruth hastened to say. "That is what I mean. My 'Brighteyes' is a full-blooded Indian maiden just like Wonota. Now, you talk with Wonota—try to get to the very heart of the girl. Then you will see."

"See what?" he demanded, staring.

"What you will see," returned Ruth, with a laugh. "Go ahead and get acquainted with Wonota. Meanwhile I will be getting this condensed plot of the story into shape for us to talk over. I must rewrite that street scene again, I fear. And, of course, we are in a hurry?"

"Always," grumbled the producer. "We must start for our Western location as soon as possible; but the New York scenes must be shot first."

It was a fine day, and the shore of the Lumano River offered a pleasant prospect for out-of-door exercise, and after he had spent more than an hour walking about with Wonota, the

Alice B. Emerson

canny Mr. Hammond obtained, he said, a "good line" on the character and capabilities of the Indian girl.

"You had me guessing for a time, Miss Ruth," he laughingly said to the girl of the Red Mill. "I did not know what you were hinting at I see it now. Wonota is a true redskin. We read about the stoicism of her race, but we do not realize what that means until we try to fathom an Indian's deeper feelings.

"I talked with her about her father. She is very proud of him, this Totantora, as she calls him. But only now and then does she express (and that in a flash) her real love and admiration for him.

"She is deeply, and justly, angered at that Dakota Joe Fenbrook. But she scarcely expresses that feeling in her face or voice. She speaks of his cruelty to her with sadness in her voice merely, and scarcely a flicker of expression in her countenance."

"Ah!" Ruth said. "Now you see what I see. It is impossible for her to register changing expressions and feelings as a white girl would. Nor would she be natural as 'Brighteyes' if she easily showed emotion. Yet she mustn't be stolid, for if she does the audience will never get what we are trying to put over."

"The director has got to have judgment—I agree to that," said Mr. Hammond, nodding. "Wonota must be handled with care. But she's got it in her to be a real star in time. She photographs like a million dollars!" and he laughed. "Now if we can teach her to be expressive enough—well, I am more than ever willing to take the chance with her, provided you, Miss Ruth, will agree to supply the vehicles of expression."

"You flatter me, Mr. Hammond," returned Ruth, flushing

faintly. "I shall of course be glad to do my best in the writing line."

"That's it. Between us we ought to make a lot of money. And incidentally to make an Indian star who will make 'em all sit up and take notice."

Ruth was so much interested in "Brighteyes" by this time that she "ate, slept, walked and talked" little else—to quote Helen. But Tom's sister grew much interested in the production, too.

"I'm going with you—to New York, anyway," she announced. "I might as well. Father is so busy with his business now that I scarcely see him from week end to week end. Dear me, if Tommy only would come home!"

"I guess he'd be delighted," rejoined Ruth, smiling. "But if you go with me, honey, you're likely to be dragged around a good deal. I expect to jump from New York to somewhere in the Northwest. Mr. Hammond has not exactly decided. The weather is very promising, and if we can shoot the outdoor scenes before Christmas we'll be all right."

"Well, I do love to travel. Maybe we could get Jennie to go, too," Helen said reflectively.

"She certainly would help," laughed Ruth. "I would rather laugh with Jennie than grouch with anybody else."

"The wisdom of Mrs. Socrates," scoffed Helen. "Anyway, Ruthie, I'll write her at once and tell her to begin pulling wires. You know, Mr. Stone is as 'sot as the everlasting hills'—and it takes something to move the hills, you know. He will have to be convinced, maybe, that Jennie's health demands a change of climate at just this time."

Alice B. Emerson

"She looks it."

"Well, one might expect her to fade away a bit because of Henri's absence. I wonder if she's heard from him since the armistice?"

"If she hasn't she'll need something besides a change of climate, I assure you," laughed Ruth again. "She hates ocean voyaging, does Jennie; but she wouldn't wait till she could go in an ox-cart to get back to France if Henri forgot to write."

There was one thing sure: Jennie Stone was a delighted host when Helen arrived in New York a few days ahead of Ruth and Wonota. Ruth had not intended to go to the Stones; she would have felt more independent at a hotel. She did not know what engagements Mr. Hammond or the director of the picture might make for her. So she tried to dodge Jennie's invitation.

When the train got in from New England, however, and Ruth and the Indian girl, following a red-capped porter with their bags, walked through the gateway of entrance to the concourse of the Grand Central Terminal, there were both Jennie and Helen waiting to spy them.

"Mr. Hammond told me to come to the Borneaux. He has made reservations there," Ruth said.

"That's all right for to-morrow," declared Jennie bruskly. "Hotel rooms are all right to make up in, or anything like that. But you are both going to my house for to-night"

"Now, Jennie—"

"No buts or ands about it!" exclaimed her friend. "If you don't come, Ruthie Fielding, I'll never speak to you again. And if Wonota doesn't come I declare I'll tell Dakota Joe where she is, and he'll come after her and steal her. In fact," Jennie added, wickedly smiling, "his old Wild West Show is playing right here in the Big Town this week."

"You don't mean it!" exclaimed Ruth, while the Indian girl shrank a little closer to her friend.

"Sure do. In Brooklyn. A three-day stand in one of the big armories over there, I believe. So a telephone call—"

"Shucks!" exclaimed Helen. "Don't you believe her, Wonota. Just the same you folks had better come to the Stone house. Mr. Stone has taken a whole box to-night for one of the very best musical shows that ever was!"

Ruth could see that the Indian girl was eager to agree. She did show some small emotions which paleface girls displayed. She laughed more than at first, too. But she was often downright gloomy when thinking of Chief Totantora.

However, seeing Wonota wished to accept the invitation, and desiring herself to please Helen and Jennie, Ruth agreed. They telephoned a message to the Hotel Borneaux and then went off to dinner at the Stone house. It was a very nice party indeed, and even busy Mr. Stone did his best to put Wonota at her ease.

"Some wigwam this, isn't it, Wonata?" said Helen, smiling, as the girls went upstairs after dinner to prepare for the theatre.

"The Osage nation does not live in wigwams, Miss Cameron," said Wonota quietly. "We are not blanket Indians and have not been for two generations."

"Well, look at the clothes you wore in that show!" cried Jennie. "That head-dress looked wild enough, I must say—

Alice B. Emerson

and those fringed leggings and all that."

Wonota smiled rather grimly. "The white people expect to see Indians in their national costumes. Otherwise it would be no novelty, would it? Why, some of the girls—Osage girls of pure blood too—at Three Rivers Station wear garments that are quite up to date. You must not forget that at least we have the catalogs from the city stores to choose from, even if we do not actually get to the cities to shop."

"Printer's ink! It is a great thing," admitted Helen. "I don't suppose there are really any wild Indians left."

The four girls and Aunt Kate were whisked in a big limousine to the play, and Wonota enjoyed the brilliant spectacle and the music as much as any of the white girls.

"Believe me," whispered Jennie to Ruth, "give any kind of girl a chance to dress up and go to places like this, and see other girls all fussed up, as your Tommy says—"

"Helen's Tommy, you mean," interposed Ruth.

"Rats!" murmured the plump girl, falling back upon Briar-wood Hall slang in her momentary disgust. "Well, anyway, Miss Fielding, what I said is so. Wonota would like to dress like the best dressed girl in the theatre, and wear ropes of pearls and a plume in her hat—see that one yonder! Isn't it superb?"

"The poor birdie that lost it," murmured Ruth.

"I declare, I don't believe you half enjoy yourself thinking of the reverse of the shield all the time," sniffed Jennie Stone. "And yet you do manage to dress pretty good yourself."

"One does not have to be bizarre to look well and

up-to-date," declared the girl of the Red Mill. "But that has nothing to do with Wonota."

"I did get off the track, didn't I?" laughed Jennie. "Oh, well! Dress her up, or any other foreign girl, in American fashion and she seems to fit into the picture all right—"

"'Foreign girl' and 'American fashion'?" gasped Ruth. "As— as *you* sometimes say, Jennie, 'how do you get that way'? Wonota is a better American than we are. Her ancestors did not have to come over in the *Mayflower*, with Henry Hudson, or with Sir Walter Raleigh."

"Isn't that a fact?" laughed Jennie. "I certainly am forgetting everything I ever learned at school. And, to tell the truth," she added, making a little face at her chum, "I feel better for it. I just *crammed* at Ardmore and Briarwood."

Helen heard this. She glanced scornfully over Jennie's still too plump figure. "I should say you did," she observed. "You used to create a famine at old Briarwood Hall, I remember. But I would not brag about it, Heavy."

"Crammed my brain, I mean," wailed the plump girl. "Can't you let me forget my avoirdupois at all?"

"It is like the poor," laughed Ruth. "It is always with us, Jennie. We cannot look at you and visualize your skeleton. You are too well upholstered."

This sort of banter did not appeal to the Indian girl. She did not, in fact, hear much of it. All her attention was given to the play on the stage and the brilliant audience. She had traveled considerably with Dakota Joe's show, but she had never seen anything like the audience in this Broadway theatre.

Alice B. Emerson

She went back to the Stone domicile in a sort of daze—smiling and happy in her quiet way, but quite speechless. Even Jennie could not "get a rise out of her," as she confessed to Helen and Ruth after they were ready for bed and the plump girl had come in to perch on one of the twin beds her chums occupied for the night.

"But I like this Osage flower," observed Jennie. "And I am just as anxious as I can be to see you make a star actress out of her, Ruthie."

"It will be Mr. Hammond and the director who do that."

"I guess you'll be in it," said Helen promptly. "If it wasn't for your story they would not be able to feature Wonota."

"Anyway," went on Jennie, "I want to go West with you, Ruth—and so does Helen. Don't you, Nell?"

"I certainly do," agreed Ruth's good friend. "Heavy and I are going to tag along, Ruthie, somehow. If there is a chaperone, father said I could go."

"Not Aunt Kate!" cried Jennie. "She says she has had enough. We dragged her down East this summer, but she will not leave Madison Avenue this winter."

"No need of worrying about that. Mother Paisley is going with the company. I have a part for her in my picture. She always looks out for the girls—a better chaperone than Mr. Hammond could hire," said Ruth.

"Fine!" cried Helen. "We'll go, then."

"We will," echoed Jennie.

"I wish you'd go to bed and let me go to sleep," complained

the girl of the Red Mill. "I have a hard day's work to-morrow—I feel it."

She was not mistaken in this feeling. At eight Mr. Hammond's assistant telephoned that the director and the company would meet Ruth and Wonota at a certain downtown corner where several of the scenes were to be shot. Dressing rooms in a neighboring hotel had been enga-ged. Ruth and her charge hastened through their breakfast, and Mr. Stone's chauffeur drove them down to the corner mentioned.

It was a very busy spot, especially about noon. Ruth had seen so much of this location work done, that it did not bother her. She was only to stand to one side and watch, anyway. But Wonota asked:

"Oh! we don't have to do this right out here in public, do we, Miss Fielding?"

"You do," laughed her friend. "Why, the people on the street help make the picture seem reasonable and natural. You need not be frightened."

"But, shall I have to be in that half-Indian costume Mr. Hammond told me to wear? What will people say—or think?"

Ruth was amused. "That's the picture. You will see some of the characters in stranger garments than those of yours before we have finished. And, anyway, in New York you often see the most outlandish costumes on people—Turks in their national dress, Hindoos with turbans and robes, Japanese and Chinese women dressed in the silks and brocades of their lands. Oh, don't worry about bead-trimmed leggings and a few feathers. And your skirt in that costume is nowhere near as short as those worn by three-fourths of the

Alice B. Emerson

girls you will see."

Aside from Wonota herself, there were few of the characters of the picture of "Brighteyes" appearing in the scenes at this point. Mr. Hammond had obtained a police permit of course, and the traffic officers and some other policemen in the neighborhood took an interest in the affair.

Traffic was held back at a certain point for a few moments so that there would not be too many people in the scene. Wonota could not be hidden. Ruth stood in the street watching the arrangements by the director and his assistants. Two films are always made at the same time, and the two camera men had got into position and had measured with their tapes the field of the picture to be taken.

Ruth had noticed an automobile stopped by the police on the other side of the cross street. She even was aware that two men in it were not dressed like ordinary city men. They had broad-brimmed hats on their heads.

But she really gave the car but a momentary glance. Wonota took up her closest attention. The Indian girl crossed and recrossed the field of the camera until she satisfied the director that her gait and facial expression was exactly what he wanted.

"All right!" he said through his megaphone. "Camera! Go!"

And at that very moment, and against the commanding gesture of the policeman governing the traffic, the car Ruth had so briefly noticed started forward, swerved into the avenue, and ran straight at Ruth as though to run her down!

CHAPTER XI

EVADING THE TRAFFIC POLICE

Ruth had turned her back on the car and did not see it slip out of the crowd of motor traffic and turn into the avenue. But Wonota, the Indian girl, saw her friend's danger. She uttered a loud cry and bounded out of the camera field just as the two camera men began to crank their machines.

"Look out, Miss Fielding!"

The cry startled Ruth, but it did not aid her much to escape. And perhaps the chauffeur of the car only intended to crowd by the girl of the Red Mill and so escape from the traffic hold-up.

At Wonota's scream the director shouted for the camera men to halt. He started himself with angry excitement after the Indian girl. She had utterly spoiled the shot.

But on the instant he was adding his warning cry to Wonota's and to the cries of other bystanders. Ruth, amazed, could not understand what Wonota meant. Then the car was upon her, the mudguard knocked her down, and her loose coat catching in some part of the car, she was dragged for several yards before Wonota could reach her.

Alice B. Emerson

Over and over in the dust Ruth had been whirled. She was breathless and bruised. She could not even cry out, the shock of the accident was so great.

The instant the Indian girl reached the prostrate Ruth the motor-car broke away and its driver shot the machine around the nearest corner and out of sight.

A policeman charged after the car at top speed, but when he reached the corner there were so many other cars in the cross street that he could not identify the one that had caused the accident.

To Ruth, Wonota gasped: "That bad man! I knew he would do something mean, but I thought it would be to me."

Ruth could scarcely reply. The director was at her side, as well as other sympathetic people. She was lifted up, but she could not stand. Something had happened to her left ankle. She could bear no weight upon it without exquisite pain.

For the time the taking of the picture was called off. The traffic officer allowed the stalled cars to pass on. A crowd began to assemble about Ruth.

"Do take me into the hotel—somewhere!" she gasped. "I—I can't walk—"

One of the camera men and the director, Mr. Hooley, made a seat with their hands, and sitting in this and with Wonota to steady her, the girl of the Red Mill was hurried under cover, leaving the throng of spectators on the street quite sure that the accident had been a planned incident of the moving picture people. They evidently considered Ruth a "stunt actress."

It was not until Ruth was alone with Wonota in a hotel room, lying on a couch, the Indian girl stripping the shoe and stocking from the injured limb, that Ruth asked what Wonota had meant when she first bounded toward her, shrieking her warning of the motor-car's approach.

"What did you mean, Wonota?" asked the girl of the Red Mill. "Who was it ran over me? I know Mr. Hooley will try to find him, but—"

"That bad, *bad* Dakota Joe!" interrupted the Indian girl with vehemence, her eyes flashing and the color deeping in her bronze cheeks. "When your friend told us he was in this city, I feared."

"Why, Wonota!" cried Ruth, sitting up in surprise, "do you mean to say that Dakota Joe Fenbrook was driving that car?"

"No. He cannot drive a car. But it was one of his men— Yes."

"I can scarcely believe it. He deliberately ran me down?"

"I saw Dakota Joe in the back of the car just as it shot down toward you, Miss Fielding. He is a bad, bad man! He was leaning forward urging that driver on. I know he was."

"Why, it seems terrible!" Ruth sighed. "Yes, that feels good on my ankle, Wonota. I do not believe it is really sprained. Oh, but it hurt at first! Wrenched, I suppose."

Jim Hooley, the director, had telephoned for Mr. Hammond, and the producer hurried to the hotel. He insisted on bringing a surgeon with him. But by the time of their arrival Ruth felt much easier, and after the medical man had pronounced no real harm done to the ankle, Ruth dressed again, insisting that a second attempt be made to shoot the scene while the sun remained high enough.

The police had endeavored to trace the motor-car that had caused the accident. But it seemed that nobody had noted the numbers on the machine, or even the kind of car it was. Ruth had forbidden Wonota to tell what she revealed to her. If it was Dakota Joe who had run her down there was no use attempting to fasten the guilt of the incident upon him unless they were positive and could prove his guilt.

"And you know, Wonota, you cannot be *sure*—"

"I saw him. It was for but a moment, but I *saw* him," said the Indian girl positively.

"Even at that, it would take corroborative testimony to convince the court," mused Ruth.

"I do not understand paleface laws," said Wonota, shaking her head. "If an Indian does something like that to another Indian, the injured one can punish his enemy. And he almost always does."

"But we cannot take the law into our own hands that way."

"Why not?" asked Wonota. "Is a redman so much superior to a white man? If the redman can punish an enemy why cannot a white man?"

"Our law does not leave it in our hands to punish," said Ruth, quietly, though rather staggered by the Indian girl's question. "We have courts, and judges, and methods of criminal procedure. A person who has been injured by another cannot be the best judge of the punishment to be meted out to the one who has harmed him."

"Why not?" demanded Wonota, promptly. "He is the one hurt. Who other than he should deal out punishment?"

Ruth was silenced for the time being. In fact, Wonota looked upon mundane matters from such a different angle that it was sometimes impossible for Ruth to convince her protege that the white man's way was better.

However, this incident gave Ruth Fielding a warning that she did not intend to ignore. A little later she told Mr. Hammond of the Indian girl's suspicion that it was Fenbrook who had been the cause of Ruth's slight injury. It was too late then to set the police on the track of the showman, for on making private inquiry Mr. Hammond found that Dakota Joe's show had already left Brooklyn and was *en route* for some city in the Middle West.

"But it seems scarcely probable, Miss Ruth," the producer said, "that that fellow would take such a chance. And to hurt *you!* Why, if he had tried to injure that Indian girl, I might be convinced. She probably saw somebody in the car with a sombrero on—"

"I noticed two men in that car with broad hats," confessed Ruth. "But I gave them only a glance. It doesn't seem very sensible to believe that the man would deliberately hurt me. Yet he did threaten us when he was angry, there at the mill. No getting around that."

Mr. Hammond shrugged his shoulders and laughed. "You will begin to believe that the making of moving pictures is a pretty perilous business."

"It may be." She laughed, yet rather doubtfully. "I am to be on the watch for the 'hand in the dark,' am I not? At any rate when we are hear Dakota Joe again, I will keep a very sharp lookout."

"Yes, of course, Miss Ruth, we'll all do that," returned Mr. Hammond, more seriously now, for he saw that Ruth was

Alice B. Emerson

really disturbed. "Still, whatever his intentions, I do not believe Fenbrook will have the power to do any real harm. At any rate, keep your courage up, for we are forewarned now, and can take care of ourselves—and of you," he added, with a smile, as he left her.

CHAPTER XII

BOUND FOR THE NORTHWEST

Because of the accident in which Ruth might have been seriously hurt, the company was delayed for a day in New York, Altogether the various shots (some of them of and in one of the tallest office buildings on Broadway) occupied more than a week—more time than Mr. Hammond wished to give to the work in the East.

Nevertheless, Ruth's finished script, as handled deftly by the continuity writer, promised so well that the producer was willing to make a special production of it. The money—and time—cost were important factors in the making of the picture; but the selection of the cast was not to be overlooked. Jim Hooley had chosen the few acting in the Eastern scenes with Wonota, including the hero, whom, to tell the truth, the Indian girl considered a rather wonderful person because she saw him in a dress suit"

"Yes, it is true! No Indian could look so heroic a figure," she whispered to Ruth. "He looks like—like a nobleman. I have read about noblemen in the book of an author named Scott—Sir Walter Scott. Noblemen must look like Mr. Albert Grand."

"And to me he looks like a head waiter," said Ruth, when

laughingly relating this to Helen and Jennie.

"Don't let Mr. Grand hear you say that," warned Helen. "They tell me that he refuses to appear in any picture where at least once he does not walk into the scene in a dress suit. He claims his clientele demand it—he looks so perfectly splendid in the 'soup and fish.'"

"Then why laugh at Wonota?" demanded Jennie Stone. "She is no more impressed by his surface qualities than are the movie fans who like Mr. Grand."

"Well, it is a great game," laughed Ruth. "Some of the movie stars have more laughable eccentricities or idiosyncracies than that. I wonder what our Wonota will develop if she becomes a star?"

The development of the Indian girl was promising so far. She had feeling for her part, if it was at first rather difficult for her to express in her features those emotions which, as an Indian, she had considered it proper to hide. She did just enough of this to make her feelings show on the screen, yet without being unnatural in the part of Brighteyes, the Indian maid.

Mr. Hammond was inclined to believe that "Brighteyes" would be a big feature picture. The director was enthusiastic about it as well. And even the camera man (than whom can be imagined no more case-hardened critic of pictures) expressed his belief that it would be a "knockout."

Mr. Hammond arranged for a special car for the cross-continent run, and he took his own family along, as the weather prophesied for the ensuing few weeks was favorable to out-of-door work and living. The special car made it possible for Ruth and her two friends, Helen and Jennie, as well as the Osage Indian girl, to be very comfortably placed during the journey.

Ruth had traveled before this—north, south, east and west—and there was scarcely anything novel in train riding for her. But a journey would never be dull with Jennie Stone and Helen Cameron as companions!

They ruined completely the morale of the car service. The colored porter could scarcely shine the other passengers' shoes he was kept so much at the beck and call of the two wealthy girls, who tipped lavishly. The Pullman conductor was cornered on every possible occasion and led into discourse entirely foreign to his duties. Even the "candy butcher" was waylaid and made to serve the ends of two girls who had perfectly idle hands and—so Ruth declared—quite as idle brains.

"Well, goodness!" remarked Helen, "we must occupy our minds and time in some way. You, Ruthie, are confined to that story of yours about twenty-five hours out of the twenty-four. Even Wonota has thought only for her tiresome beadwork when she is not studying her part with Mr. Hooley and you. I know we'll have fun when we get to the Hubbell Ranch where Mr. Hammond says your picture is to be filmed. I do just dote on cowboys and the fuzzy little ponies they ride."

"And the dear cows!" drawled Jennie. "Do you remember that maniacal creature that attacked our motor-car that time we went to Silver Ranch, years and years and years ago? You know, back in the Paleozoic Age!"

"Quite so," agreed Helen. "I have a photographic remembrance of that creature—ugh! And how he burst our tires!"

"He, forsooth! What a way to speak of a cow!"

"It wasn't a cow; it was a steer," declared Helen confidently.

Ruth retired from the observation platform where her chums were ensconced, allowing them to argue the matter to a finish. It was true that the girl of the Red Mill was very busy most of her waking hours on the train. They all took a recess at Chicago, however, and it was there a second incident occurred that showed Dakota Joe Fenbrook had not forgotten his threat to "get even" with Ruth Fielding and the moving picture producer with whom she was associated.

The special car was sidetracked just outside of Chicago and the whole party motored into the city in various automobiles and on various errands. The Hammonds had relatives to visit. Ruth and her three girl companions had telegraphed ahead for reservations at one of the big hotels, and they proposed to spend the two days and nights Mr. Hammond had arranged for in seeing the sights and attending two particular theatrical performances.

"And I declare!" cried Helen, as they rolled on through one of the suburbs of the city, "there is one of the sights, sure enough. See that billboard, girls?"

"Oh!" cried Wonota, who possessed quite as sharp eyes as anybody in the party.

"We can't escape that man," sighed Jennie, as she read in towering letters the announcement of "Dakota Joe's Wild West and Frontier Round-Up."

"I am sorry the show is here in Chicago," added Ruth with serious mien. "I am still limping. Next time that awful man will manage to lame me completely."

"You ought to have a guard. Tell the police—do!" exclaimed Jennie Stone.

"Tell the police *what?*" demanded Ruth, with scorn. "We can't prove anything."

"I know it was Joe in that car that ran you down, Miss Fielding," declared Wonota, with anxiety.

"Yes. But nobody else saw him—to recognize him, I mean. We cannot base a complaint upon such little foundation. Nor would it be well, perhaps, to get Dakota Joe into the courts. He is a very vindictive man—he must be—"

"He is very bad man!" repeated Wonota vehemently.

"Yes. That is just it. Why stir up his passions to a greater degree, then?"

"Of course, Ruthie would want to turn 'the other cheek,'" scoffed Jennie.

"I am not going around with a chip on my shoulder, looking for somebody to knock it off," laughed the girl of the Red Mill. "I just want Joe to leave us alone—that's all."

Wonota shook her head and seemed unconvinced of the wisdom of this. She was not a pacifist. She knew, too, the heart of the showman, and perhaps she feared him more than she was willing to tell her new friends.

The four girls made their headquarters at the hotel, and then set forth at once to shop and to look. As the hours of that first day passed Wonota was vastly excited over the new sights. For once she lost that stoic calmness which was her racial trait. The big stores and the tall buildings here in the mid-western city seemed to impress her even more than had those in New York.

There was reason for that. She was, while in New York, so

Alice B. Emerson

much taken up with the part she was playing in "Brighteyes" that she could think of little else. She saw many things in the stores she wished to buy. Ruth had advanced Wonota some money on her contract with the Alectrion Film Corporation. But when it came right down to the point of buying the things that girls like and long for—little trinkets and articles of adornment—the Indian girl hesitated.

"Buy it if it pleases you," Ruth said, rather wondering at the firmness with which Wonota drew back from selecting and paying for something that cost less than a dollar.

"No, Miss Fielding. Wonota does not need that. Chief Totantora may be lost to me forever. I should not adorn myself, or think of self-adornment. No! I will save my money until I can go to that Europe where the great chief is held a prisoner."

The girls—Helen and Jennie—were both for buying presents for the Indian girl, as she would not use her own money. But Ruth would not allow them to purchase other than the simplest souveniers.

"That would spoil it all. Let her deny herself in such a cause—it will not hurt her," the girl of the Red Mill said sensibly. "She has an object in life and should be encouraged to follow out her plan for helping Chief Totantora."

"Maybe he is not alive now," said Helen, thoughtfully.

"I would not suggest that," Ruth hastened to rejoin. "As long as she can hope, the better for Wonota. And I should not want her to find out that Totantora has died in captivity, before my picture is finished."

"Whoo!" breathed Jennie. "You sound sort of selfish, Ruthie Fielding."

"For her sake as well as for the sake of the picture," returned the other practically. "I tell you Wonota has got it in her to be a valuable asset to the movies. But I hope nothing will happen to make her fall down on this first piece of work. Like Mr. Hammond, I hope that she will develop into an Indian star of the very first magnitude."

Alice B. Emerson

CHAPTER XIII

DAKOTA JOE MAKES A DEMAND

At first Ruth and her friends did not worry about the presence of Fenbrook and his Wild West Show in Chicago.

"Just riding past the billboard of the show isn't going to hurt us," chuckled Jennie Stone.

It was a fact soon proved, however, that the Westerner had made it his business in some way to keep track of the movements of Wonota and her friends. He made this known to them in a most unexpected way, Mr. Hammond called Ruth up at her hotel.

"I must warn you, Miss Fielding" he said, "that I had a very unpleasant meeting with that man, Fenbrook, only an hour ago. He actually had the effrontery to look me up here in Wabash Avenue where I am staying with my family, and practically demanded that I help finance his miserable show because I had taken Wonota from him. He claims now she was his chief attraction, though he would not admit that she was worth a living wage when he had her under contract He was so excited and threatening that I called an officer and had him put out of the house."

"Oh!" murmured Ruth. "Then he is in jail? He will not

trouble us, then?"

"He is not in jail. I made no complaint. Just warned him to keep away from here. But he said something about finding Wonota and making trouble."

"I am sure, Mr. Hammond," said Ruth with no little anxiety, "that we had better leave Chicago, then, as soon as possible. And if he comes here to the hotel I will try to have him arrested and kept by the police. I am afraid of him.

"I do not believe he will do anything very desperate—"

"I am not so sure," Ruth interrupted. "Wonota is confident it was he who ran me down in New York. I am afraid of him," she repeated.

"Well, I will arrange for the shortening of our stay here. Mr. Hooley will 'phone you the time we will leave—probably to-morrow morning very early."

Ruth said nothing to the other three girls—why trouble them with a mere possibility?—and they went to the theatre that evening and enjoyed the play immensely. But getting out of the taxicab at the hotel door near midnight, Wonota, who was the first to step out, suddenly crowded back into Ruth Fielding's arms as the latter attempted to follow her to the sidewalk.

"What is the matter, Wonota?" the girl of the Red Mill asked.

"There he is!" murmured the Indian girl, drawing herself up.

"There who is?" was Ruth's demand. Then she saw the object of Wonota's anxiety, Dakota Joe stood under the portico of the hotel entrance. "He's waiting for us!" hissed Ruth. "Stop, girls! Don't get out."

Alice B. Emerson

Helen and Jennie, over the heads of the others, saw the man. Jennie was irrepressible of course.

"What do you expect us to do? Ride around all night in this taxi?"

"Call a policeman!" cried Helen, under her breath.

"Come back in here, Wonota," commanded Ruth, making up her mind with her usual assurance. "Say nothing, girls." Then to the driver Ruth observed: "Isn't there a side entrance to this hotel?"

"Yes, ma'am. Round on the other street."

"Take us around to that door. We see somebody waiting here whom we do not wish to speak with."

"All right, ma'am," agreed the taxicab driver.

In two minutes they were whisked around to the other door, and entered the hotel thereby. As they passed through the lobby to the elevators one of the clerks came to Ruth.

"A man has been asking for you, Miss Fielding" he said. "He—he seems a peculiar individual—"

Ruth described Dakota Joe Fenbrook and the clerk admitted that he was the man. "A rather rude person," he said.

"So rude that we do not wish to see him," Ruth told the clerk. "Please keep him away from us. He is annoying, and if he attempts to interfere with me, I will call a policeman."

"Oh, we could allow nothing like that," the clerk hastened to say. "No disturbance would be countenanced by the management of the hotel," and he shook his head. "We will keep him away from you, Miss Fielding."

"Thank you," said Ruth, and followed her friends into the elevator. She felt that they were free of Dakota Joe until morning at least She assured Wonota that she need not worry.

"That bad man may hurt you. I am not afraid," declared the Indian girl. "If I only had him out on the Osage Reservation, I would know what to do to with him."

But she did not explain what treatment she would accord Dokota Joe if she were at home.

It was only seven o'clock when Jim Hooley called on the telephone and told Ruth that, following instructions from Mr. Hammond, he had gathered the company together and that the special car standing in the railroad yard outside Chicago would be picked up by the nine-thirty western bound Continental. The girls had scarcely time to dress and drive to the point of departure. There was some "scrabbling," as Jennie expressed it, to dress, get their possessions together, and get away from the hotel.

"Didn't see Dakota Joe anywhere about, did you?" Helen asked, as their taxi-cab-left the hotel entrance.

"For goodness' sake! he would not have hung about the hotel all night, would he?" demanded Jennie.

"Mr. Hammond seems to be afraid of the man" pursued Helen. "Or we would not be running away like this."

Ruth smiled. "I guess," she said, "that Mr. Hammond is hurrying us on for a different reason. You must remember that he has this company on salary and that the longer we delay on the way to the Hubbell Ranch the more money it is

Alice B. Emerson

costing him while the company is idle."

It was proved, however, that the picture producer had a good reason for wishing to get out of Dakota Joe's neighborhood. When the four girls in the taxicab rolled up to the gate of the railroad yard and got out with their bags, Dakota Joe himself popped out of hiding. With him a broad-hatted man in a blue suit.

"Hey!" ejaculated the showman, standing directly in Ruth's path. "I got you now where I want you. That Hammond man won't help me, and I told him the trouble I'm in jest because he got that Injun gal away from me. I see her! That's the gal—"

"What do you want of me, Mr. Fenbrook?" demanded Ruth, bravely, and gesturing Wonota to remain behind her. "I have no idea why you should hound me in this way."

"I ain't houndin' you."

"I should like to know what you call it then!" the girl of the Red Mill demanded indignantly.

She was quick to grasp the chance of engaging Fenbrook in an argument that would enable Wonota and the two other girls to slip out of the other door of the taxicab and reach the yard gate. She flashed a look over her shoulder that Helen Cameron understood. She and Jennie and Wonota alighted from the other side of the cab.

"I got an officer here," stammered Dakota Joe. "He's a marshal. That Injun gal's got to be taken before the United States District Court. She's got to show cause why she shouldn't come back to my show and fill out the time of her contract."

"She finished her contract with you, and you know it, Fenbrook," declared Ruth, turning to pay the driver of the cab.

"I say she didn't!" cried Dakota Joe. "Officer! You serve that warrant—Hey! where's that Wonota gone to?"

The Indian girl and Ruth's friends had disappeared. Dakota Joe lunged for the gate. But since the beginning of the war this particular railroad yard had been closed to the public. A man stood at the gate who barred the entrance of the showman.

"You don't come in here, brother," said the railroad man. "Not unless you've got a pass or a permit."

"Hey!" shouted Dakota Joe, calling the marshal. "Show this guy your warrant."

"Don't show me nothin'," rejoined the railroad employee. He let Ruth slip through and whispered: "Your party's aboard your car. There's a switcher coupled on. She'll scoot you all down the yard to the main line. Get aboard."

Ruth slipped through the gate, while the guard stood in a position to prevent the two men from approaching it. The girl heard the gate close behind her.

It was evident that Mr. Hammond had been apprised of Dakota Joe's attempt to bring the Indian girl into court. Of course, the judge would deny his appeal; but a court session would delay the party's journey westward.

Ruth saw the other girls ahead of her, and she ran to the car. Mr. Hammond himself was on the platform to welcome them.

"That fellow is a most awful nuisance. I had to make an arrangement with the railroad company to get us out of here at once. Luckily I have a friend high up among the officials of the company. Come aboard, Miss Ruth. Everybody else is here and we are about to start."

CHAPTER XIV

THE HUBBELL RANCH

"You see, Miss Ruth," Mr. Hammond told the girl of the Red Mill as the special car rolled out of the railroad yard, "this Dakota Joe has become a very annoying individual. We had to fairly run away from him."

"I do not understand," Ruth said. "I think he should be shown his place—and that place I believe is the police station."

"It would be rather difficult to get him into that for any length of time. And in any case," and the picture producer smiled, it would cost more than it would be worth. He really has done nothing for which he can be punished—"

"I don't know. He might have had me killed that time his auto ran me down," interrupted Ruth, indignantly.

"But the trouble is, we cannot prove that," Mr. Hammond hastened to repeat. "I will see that you are fully protected from him hereafter."

Mr. Hammond did not realize what a large undertaking that was to be. But he meant it at the time.

"The man is in trouble—no doubt of it," went on the

Alice B. Emerson

producer reflectively. "He has had a bad season, and his winter prospects are not bright. I gave him an hour of my time yesterday before I advised you that we would better get away from Chicago."

"But what does he expect of you, Mr. Hammond?" asked Ruth in surprise.

"He claims we are the cause of his unhappy business difficulties. His show in on the verge of disintegrating. He wanted me to back him with several thousand dollars. Of course, that is impossible."

"Why!" cried Ruth, "I would not risk a cent with such a man."

"I suppose not. And I felt no urge to comply with his request. He was really so rough about it, and became so ugly, that I had to have him shown out of the house."

"Goodness! I am glad we are going far away from him."

"Yes, he is not a nice neighbor," agreed Mr. Hammond. "I hope Wonota will repay us for all the bother we have had with Dakota Joe."

"It seems too bad. Of course, it is not Wonota's fault," said Ruth. "But if we had not come across her—if I had not met her, I mean—you would not have been annoyed in this way, Mr. Hammond."

"Take it the other way around, Miss Ruth," returned her friend, with a quizzical smile. "We should be very glad that you did meet Wonota. Considering what that mad bull would have done to you if she had not swerved him by a rifle shot, a little bother like this is a small price to pay."

"Oh—well!"

"In addition," said Mr. Hammond briskly, "look what we may make out of the Indian girl. She may coin us a mint of money, Ruth Fielding."

"Perhaps," smiled Ruth.

But she was not so eager for money. The thing that fascinated her imagination was the possibility that they might make of Wonota, the Osage maiden, a great and famous movie star. Ruth desired very much to have a part in that work.

She knew, because Mr. Hammond had told her, as well as Wonota herself, that the Osage Indians as a tribe were the wealthiest people under the guardianship of the American Government. Their oil leases were fast bringing the tribe a great fortune. But Wonota, being under age, had no share in this wealth. At this time the income of the tribe was between four and five thousand dollars a day—and the tribe was not large.

"But Wonota can have none of that," explained the Indian maid. "It is apportioned to the families, and Totantora, the head of my family, is somewhere in that Europe where the war is. I can get no share of the money. It is not allowed."

So, with the incentive of getting money for her search, Wonota was desirous of pleasing her white friends in every particular. Besides, ambition had budded in the girl's heart. She wanted to be a screen actress.

"If your 'Brighteyes,' Miss Fielding, is ever shown at Three Rivers Station or Pawhuska, where the Agency is, I know every member of the tribe will go to see the film. When some of the young men of our tribe acted in a round-up picture when I was a little girl, even the old men and great-grandmothers traveled a hundred miles to see the film run off. It was like an exodus, for some of them were two days and nights on the way"

"The Osage Indians are not behind the times, then?" laughed Ruth. "They are movie fans?"

"They realize that their own day has departed. The buffalo and elk have gone. Even the prairie chickens are seen but seldom. Almost no game is found upon our plains, and not much back in the hills. Many of our young men till the soil. Some have been to the Carlisle School and have taken up professions or are teachers. The Osage people are no longer warlike. But some of our young men volunteered for this white man's war."

"I know that," sad Ruth warmly. "I saw some of them over there in France—at least, some Indian volunteers. Captain Cameron worked in the Intelligence Service with some of them. That is the spy service, you know. The Indians were just as good scouts in France and Belgium as they were on their own plains."

"We are always the same. It is only white men who change," declared Wonota with confidence. "The redman is never two-faced or two-tongued."

"Well," grumbled Jennie, afterward, "what answer was there to make to that? She has her own opinion of Lo, the poor Indian, and it would be impossible to shake it."

"Who wants to shake it?" demanded Helen. "Maybe she is right, at that!"

The thing about Wonota that "gave the fidgets" to Jennie and Helen was the fact that she could sit for mile after mile, while the train rocked over the rails, beading moccasins and other wearing apparel, and with scarcely a glance out of the car window. Towns, villages, rivers, plains, woods and hills, swept by in green and brown panorama, and seemed to interest Wonota not at all. It was only when the train, after they changed at Denver, began to climb into the Rockies that the Indian maid grew interested.

The Osage Indians had always been a plains' tribe. The rugged and white-capped heights interested Wonota because they were strange to her. Here, too, were primeval forests visible from the windows of the car. Hemlock and spruce in black masses clothed the mountainsides, while bare-limbed groves of other wood filled the valleys and the sweeps of the hills.

Years before Ruth and her two chums had been through this country in going to "Silver Ranch," but the charm of its mysterious gorges, its tottering cliffs, its deep canyons where the dashing waters flowed, and the generally rugged aspect of all nature, did not fail now to awe them. Wonota was not alone in gazing, enthralled, at the landscape which was here revealed.

Two days of this journey amid the mountains, and the train slowed down at Clearwater, where the special car was sidetracked. Although the station was some distance from the "location" Mr. Hammond's representative had selected for the taking of the outdoor pictures, the company was to use the car as its headquarters. There were several automobiles and a herd of riding ponies at hand for the use of the company. Here, too, Mr. Hammond and his companions were met by the remainder of the performers selected to play parts in "Brighteyes."

There were about twenty riders—cowpunchers and the like; "stunt riders," for the most part. In addition there were more

Alice B. Emerson

than a score of Indians—some pure blood like Wonota, but many of them halfbreeds, and all used to the moving picture work, down to the very toddlers clinging to their mothers' blankets. The Osage princess was inclined to look scornfully at this hybrid crew at first. Finally, however, she found them to be very decent sort of folk, although none of them were of her tribe.

Ruth and Helen and Jennie met several riders who had worked for Mr. Hammond when he had made Ruth's former Western picture which is described in "Ruth Fielding in the Saddle," and the gallant Westerners were ready to devote themselves to the entertainment of the girls from the East.

There was only one day of planning and making ready for the picture, in which Helen and Jennie could be "beaued" about by the cow-punchers. Ruth was engaged with Mr. Hammond, Jim Hooley, and the camera man and their assistants. Everyone was called for work on the ensuing morning and the automobiles and the cavalcade of pony-riders started for the Hubbell Ranch.

Wonota rode in costume and upon a pony that was quite the equal of her own West Wind. This pet she had shipped from the Red Mill to her home in Oklahoma before going to New York. The principal characters had made up at the car and went out in costume, too, They had to travel about ten miles to the first location.

The Hubbell Ranch grazed some steers; but It was a horse ranch in particular. The country was rugged and offered not very good pasturage for cattle. But the stockman, Arad Hubbell, was one of the largest shippers of horses and mules in the state.

It was because of the many half-broken horses and mules to be had on the ranch that Mr. Hammond had decided to make

"Brighteyes" here. The first scenes of the prologue—including the Indian scare—were to be taken in the open country near the ranch buildings. Naturally the buildings were not included in any of the pictures.

A train of ten emigrant wagons, drawn by mules, made an imposing showing as it followed the dusty cattle trail. The train wound in and out of coulees, through romantic-looking ravines, and finally out upon the flat grass-country where the Indians came first into view of the supposedly frightened pilgrims.

Helen and Jennie, as well as Ruth herself, in the gingham and sunbonnets of the far West of that earlier day, added to the crowd of emigrants riding in the wagons. When the Indians were supposed to appear the excitement of the players was very realistic indeed, and this included the mules! The stock was all fresh, and the excitement of the human performers spread to it. The wagons raced over the rough trail in a way that shook up severely the girls riding in them.

"Oh—oo!" squealed Jennie Stone, clinging to Ruth and Helen. "What *are* they trying to do? I'll be one m-a-ass of bruises!"

"Stop, William!" commanded Ruth, trying to make the driver of their wagon hear her. "This is too—too realistic."

The man did not seem to hear her at all. Ruth scrambled up and staggered toward the front, although Mr. Hooley had instructed the girls to remain at the rear of the wagons so that they could be seen from the place where the cameras were stationed.

"Stop!" cried Ruth again. "You will tip us over—or something."

Alice B. Emerson

There was good reason why William did not obey. His six mules had broken away from his control entirely.

A man must be a master driver to hold the reins over three span of mules; and William was as good as any man in the outfit. But as he got his team into a gallop the leaders took fright at the charging Indians on pony-back, and tried to leave the trail.

William was alone on the driver's seat. He put all his strength into an attempt to drag the leaders back into the trail and— the rein broke!

Under ordinary circumstances this accident would not have been of much moment. But to have pulled the other mules around, and so throw the runaways, would have spoiled the picture. William was too old a movie worker to do that.

When Ruth stumbled to the front of the swaying wagon and seized his shoulder he cast rather an embarrassed glance back at her.

"Stop them! Stop!" the girl commanded.

"I'd like mighty well to do it, Miss Fielding," said William, wagging his head, "but these dratted mules have got their heads and—they—ain't—no notion o' stoppin' this side of the ranch corrals."

Ruth understood him. She stared straight ahead with a gaze that became almost stony. This leading wagon was heading for the break of a ravine into which the trail plunged at a sharp angle. If the mules were swerved at the curve the heavy wagon would surely overturn.

In twenty seconds the catastrophe would happen!

CHAPTER XV

PURSUING DANGER

When a mule is once going, it is just as stubborn about stopping as it is about being started if it feels balky. The leading span attached to the covered wagon in which Ruth and her two chums, Helen Cameron and Jennie Stone, rode had now communicated their own fright to the four other animals. All six were utterly unmanageable.

"Do tell him to stop, Ruth!" shrieked Jennie Stone from the rear of the wagon.

The next moment she shot into the air as the wheels on one side bounced over an outcropping boulder. She came down clawing at Helen to save herself from flying out of the end of the wagon.

"Oh! This is too much!" shouted Helen, quite as frightened as her companion. "I mean to get out! Don't a-a-ask me to—to act in moving pictures again. I never will!"

"Talk about rough stuff!" groaned Jennie. "This is the limit."

Neither of them realized the danger that threatened. Of the three girls only Ruth knew what was just ahead. The maddened mules were dragging the emigrant wagon for a

Alice B. Emerson

pitch into the ravine that boded nothing less than disaster for all.

In the band of Indians riding for the string of covered wagons Wonota had been numbered. She could ride a barebacked pony as well as any buck in the party. She had removed her skirt and rode in the guise of a young brave. The pinto pony she bestrode was speedy, and the Osage maid managed him perfectly.

Long before the train of wagons and the pursuing band of Indians got into the focus of the cameras, Wonota, as well as her companions, saw that the six mules drawing the head wagon were out of control. The dash of the frightened animals added considerable to the realism of the picture, as they swept past Jim Hooley and his camera men; but the director was quite aware that disaster threatened William's outfit.

"Crank it up! Crank it!" he commanded the camera men. "It looks as if we were going to get something bigger than we expected."

Mr. Hammond stood behind him. He saw the three white girls in the rear of the wagon. It was he who shouted:

"That runaway must be stopped! It's Miss Fielding and her friends in that wagon. Stop them!"

"Great Scott, Boss! how you going to stop those mules?" Jim Hooley demanded.

But Wonota did not ask anybody as to the method of stopping the runaway. She was perfectly fearless—of either horses or mules. She lashed her pinto ahead of the rest of the Indian band, cut across a curve of the trail, and bore down on the runaway wagon.

"That confounded girl is spoiling the shot!" yelled Hooley.

"Never mind! Never mind!" returned Mr. Hammond. "She is going to do something. There!"

And Wonota certainly did do something. Aiming her pinto across the noses of the lead-mules, she swerved them off the trail before they reached that sharp turn at the break of the rough hill. The broken rein made it impossible for the driver to swerve the leaders that way; but Wonota turned the trick.

William stood up, despite the bounding wagon, his foot on the brake, yanking with all his might at the jaws of the other four mules. All six swung in a wide circle. But William admitted that it was the Indian girl who started the crazed mules into this path.

The wheels dipped and bounced, threatening each moment to capsize the wagon. But the catastrophe did not occur. The other Indians rode down upon the head of the string of wagons madly, with excited whoops. For once the whole crowd forgot that they were making a picture.

And that very forgetfulness on the part of the actors made the picture a great success The finish was not quite as Ruth had written the story, or as Hooley had planned to take it. But it was better!

"It's a peach! It's a peach! The shot was perfect!" the director cried, smiting Mr. Hammond on the back in his excitement. "What do you know about that, Boss? Can't we let her stand as the camera has it?"

"I believe it is a good shot," agreed Mr. Hammond. "We'll try it out to-night in the car." One end of the special car was arranged as a projection room. "If the Indians did not hide

Alice B. Emerson

the wagon too much, that dash of the girl was certainly spectacular."

"It was a peach," again declared the director. "And nobody will ever see that she is a girl instead of a man. We got one good shot, here, Mr. Hammond, whether anything else comes out right or not."

The girls who had taken the parts of emigrant women in the runaway wagon were not quite so enthusiastic over the success of the event, not even when the director sent his congratulations to them. All three were determined that if a "repeat" was demanded, they would refuse to play the parts again.

"I don't want to ride in anything like that wagon again," declared Ruth. "It was awful."

"Enough is enough," agreed Helen. "Another moment, and we would have been out on our heads."

"I'm black and blue—or will be—from collar to shoes. *What* a jouncing we did get! Girls, do you suppose that fellow with the shaggy ears did it on purpose?"

"Whom do you mean—William or one of the mules?" asked Helen.

"I am sure William was helpless," said Ruth. "He was just as much scared as we were. But Wonota was just splendid!"

"I am willing to pass her a vote of thanks," groaned Jennie. "But we can't expect her to be always on hand to save us from disaster. You don't catch me in any such jam again."

"Oh, nothing like this is likely to happen to us again," Ruth said. "We're just as safe taking this picture as we would be at home—at the Red Mill, for instance."

"I don't know about that," grumbled Helen. "I feel that more trouble is hanging over us. I feel it in my bones."

"You'd better get a new set of bones," said Ruth cheerfully. "Yours seem to be worse, even, than poor Aunt Alvira's."

"Nell believes that life is just one thing after another," chuckled Jennie Stone. "Having struck a streak of bad luck, it *must* keep up."

"You wait and see," proclaimed Helen Cameron, decisively nodding her head.

"That's the easiest thing in the world to do—*wait*," gibed Ruth.

"No, it isn't, either. It's the hardest thing to do," declared Jennie, and Ruth thought she could detect a shade of sadness in the light tone the plump girl adopted. "And especially when—as Nell predicts—we are waiting for some awful disaster. Huh—" and the girl shuddered as realistically as perfect health and unshaken nerves and good nature would permit—"are we to pass our lives under the shadow of impending peril?"

It did seem, however, as though Helen had come under the mantle of some seeress of old. Jennie flatly declared that "Nell must be a descendant of the Witch of Endor."

The company managed to make several scenes that day without further disaster. Although in taking a close-up of the charging Indian chief one of the camera men was knocked down by the rearing pony the chief rode, and a perfectly good two hundred dollar camera was smashed beyond hope of repair.

Alice B. Emerson

"It's begun," said Helen, ruefully. "You see!"

"If you have brought a hoodoo into this outfit, woe be it to you!" cried Ruth.

"It is not me," proclaimed her chum. "But I tell you *something* is going to happen."

They worked so late that it was night before the company took the trail for Clearwater Station. There was no moon, and the stars were veiled by a haze that perhaps foreboded a storm.

This coming storm probably was what caused the excitement in a horse herd that they passed when half way to the railroad line. Or it might have been because the motor-cars, of which there were four, were strange to the half-wild horses that the bunch became frightened.

"There's something doing with them critters, boys!" William, who was riding ahead, called back to the other pony riders, who were rear guard to the automobiles. "Keep yer eyes peeled!"

His advice was scarcely necessary. The thunder of horse-hoofs on the turf was not to be mistaken. Through the darkness the stampeding animals swept down upon the party.

"Git, you fellers!" yelled another rider. "And keep a-goin'! Jest split the wind for the station!"

The horsemen swept past the jouncing motor-cars. Some of the women in the cars screamed. Helen cried:

"What did I tell you!"

"Don't—*dare*—tell us anything more!" jerked out Jennie.

Through the murk the girls saw the heads and flaunted manes of the coming horses. Just what harm they might do to the motor-cars, which could not be driven rapidly on this rough trail, Ruth and her two chums did not know. But the threat of the wild ponies' approach was not to be ignored.

Alice B. Emerson

CHAPTER XVI

NEWS AND A THREAT

A stampede of mad cattle is like the charge of a blind and insane monster. River, nor ravine, nor any other obstruction can halt the mad rush of the horned beasts. They pile right into it, and only if it is too steep or too high do they split and go around.

A stampede of horses is different in that the equine brain appreciates danger more clearly than that of the sullen steer. Behind a cattle stampede is often left an aftermath of dead and crippled beasts. But horses are more canny. A wild horse seldom breaks a leg or suffers other injury. It is not often that the picked skeleton of a horse is found in the hills.

This herd belonging to the Hubbell ranch charged through the night directly across the trail along which the moving picture company was riding. Those on horseback could probably escape; but the motor-cars could not be driven very rapidly over the rough road.

The girls screamed as the cars bumped and jounced. Out of the darkness appeared the up-reared heads and tossing manes of the ponies. There were possibly three hundred in the herd, and they ran *en masse,* snorting and neighing, mad with that fear of the unknown which is always at the root of every stampede.

The automobile in which Ruth Fielding and her two friends, Helen and Jennie, were seated was the last of the string. It seemed as though it could not possibly escape the stampede of half-wild ponies, even if the other cars did.

"Get down in the car, girls!" shouted Ruth, suiting her action to her word. "Don't try to jump or stand up. Stoop!"

There was good reason for her command. The plunging horses seemed almost upon the car. Indeed one leader—a big black stallion,—snorting and blowing, jumped over the rear of the car, clearing it completely, and bounded away upon the other side of the trail.

He was ahead of the main stampede, however. All that found the motor-car in the path could not perform his feat. Some would be sure to plunge into the car where Ruth and Helen and Jennie crouched.

Suddenly there rode into view, coming from the head of the string of cars, a wild rider, plying whip and heel to maddened pinto pony.

"Wonota! Go back! You'll be killed!" shrieked Ruth. And then she added: "The picture will be ruined if you are hurt."

Even had the Indian girl heard Ruth's cry she would have given it small attention. Wonota was less fearful of the charging ponies than were the punchers and professional riders working for Mr. Hammond.

At least, she was the first to visualize the danger threatening the girls in the motor-car, and she did not wait to be told what to do. Up ahead the men were shouting and telling each other that Miss Fielding was in danger. But Wonota went at

Alice B. Emerson

the charging horses without question.

She forced her snorting pinto directly between the motor-car and the stampede. She lashed the foremost horses across their faces with her quirt. She wheeled her mount and kept on beside the motor-car as its driver tried to speed up along the trail.

The mad herd seemed intent on keeping with the motor-train. Wonota gave the pinto his head and lent her entire attention to striking at the first horses in the stampede. Her quirt brought squeals of pain from more than one of the charging animals.

She fell in behind the car at last, and the scattering members of the stampede swept by. Back charged several of the pony riders, but too late to give any aid. The chauffeur of Ruth's car slackened his dangerous pace and yelled:

"It's all over, you fellers! We might have been trod into the ground for all of you. It takes this Injun gal to turn the trick. I take off my hat to Wonota."

"I guess we all take off our hats to her!" cried Helen, sitting up again. "She saved us—that is what she did!"

"Good girl, Wonota!" Ruth exclaimed, as the snorting pinto brought its rider up beside the motor-car again.

"It was little to do," the Indian girl responded modestly. "After all you have done for me, Miss Fielding. And I am not afraid of horses."

"Them horses was something to be afraid of—believe me!" ejaculated one of the men. "The gal's a peach of a rider at that."

Here Helen suddenly demanded to know where Jennie was.

"I do believe she's burrowed right through the bottom of this tonneau!"

"Haven't either!" came in the muffled voice of the fleshy girl, and she began to rise up from under enveloping robes. "Take your foot off my arm, Nell. You're trampling me awfully. I thought it was one of those dreadful horses!"

"Well—I—like—that!" gasped Helen.

"I didn't," Jennie groaned, finally coming to the surface—like a porpoise, Ruth gigglingly suggested, to breathe! "I was sure one of those awful creatures was stamping on me. If I haven't suffered *this* day! Such spots as were not already black and blue, are now properly bruised. I shall be a sight."

"Poor Heavy!" said Ruth. "You always have the hard part. But, thank goodness, we escaped in safety!"

"Do let's go to a hotel somewhere and stay a week to recuperate," begged the fleshy girl, as they rode on toward the railroad town. "One day of movie making calls for a week of rest—believe me!"

"You and Helen can remain at the car—"

"Not me!" cried Helen Cameron. "I do not wish to be in the picture again, but I want to see it made."

After they arrived at the special car, where a piping hot supper was ready for them, the girls forgot the shock of their adventure. Jennie, however, groaned whenever she moved.

"'Tis too bad that fat girl got so bunged up," observed one of the punchers to Helen Cameron. "I see she's a-sufferin'."

Alice B. Emerson

"Miss Stone's avoirdupois is forever making her trouble," laughed Helen, rather wickedly.

"Huh?" demanded the man. "Alfy Dupoy? Who's that? Her feller?"

"Oh, dear me, no!" gasped Helen. "*His* name is Henri Marchand. I shall have to tell her that."

"Needn't mind," returned the man. "I can't be blamed for misunderstanding half what you Easterners say. You got me locoed right from the start."

The joke had to be told when the three friends retired that night, and it was perhaps fortunate that Jennie Stone possessed an equable disposition.

"I am the butt of everybody's joke," she said, complacently. "That is what makes me so popular. You see, you skinny girls are scarcely noticed. It is me the men-folk give their attention to."

"Isn't it nice to be so perfectly satisfied with one's self?" observed Helen, scornfully. "Come on, Ruthie! Let's sleep on that."

There were other topics to excite the friends in the morning, even before the company got away for the "location." Mail which had followed them across the continent was brought up from the post-office to the special car. Helen and Ruth were both delighted to receive letters from Captain Tom.

In the one to Ruth the young man acknowledged the receipt of her letter bearing on the matter of Chief Totantora. He said that news of the captured Wild West performers had drifted through the lines long before the armistice, and that he had now set in motion an inquiry which might yield some important news of the missing Osage chieftain—if he was yet alive—before many weeks. As for his own return, Tom could not then state anything with certainty.

*   *   *   *   *

"Nobody seems to know," he wrote. "It is all on the knees of the gods—and a badgered War Department. But perhaps I shall be with you, dear Ruth, before long."

*   *   *   *   *

Ruth did not show her letter to her girl friends. Jennie had received no news from Henri, and this disaster troubled her more than her bruised flesh. She went around with a sober face for at least an hour—which was a long time for Jennie Stone to be morose.

William, the driver who had handled the emigrant wagon the day before, came along as the men were saddling the ponies for the ride out to the ranch. He had an open letter in his hand that he had evidently just received.

"Say!" he drawled, "didn't I hear something about you taking this Injun gal away from Dakota Joe's show? Ain't that so, Miss Fielding?"

"Her contract with that man ran out and Mr. Hammond hired her," Ruth explained.

"And that left the show flat in Chicago?" pursued William.

"It was in Chicago the last we saw of it," agreed Ruth. "But Wonota had left Dakota Joe's employ long before that— while the show was in New England."

"Wal, I don't know how that is," said William. "I got a letter

Alice B. Emerson

from a friend of mine that's been ridin' with Dakota Joe. He says the show's done busted and Joe lays it to his losing this Injun gal. Joe's a mighty mean man. He threatens to come out here and bust up this whole company," and William grinned.

"You want to tell Mr. Hammond that," said Ruth, shortly.

"I did," chuckled William. "But he don't seem impressed none. However, Miss Fielding, I want to say that Dakota Joe has done some mighty mean tricks in his day. Everybody knows him around here—yes, ma'am! If he comes here, better keep your eyes open."

CHAPTER XVII

THE PROLOGUE IS FINISHED

"We must do something very nice for Wonota," Helen Cameron said seriously. "She has twice within a few hours come to our succor. I feel that we might all three have been seriously injured had she not turned the mules yesterday, and frightened off those mad horses on the trail last evening."

"'Seriously injured,' forsooth!" grumbled Jennie Stone. "What do you mean? Didn't I show you my bruises? I was seriously injured as it was! But I admit I feel grateful— heartily grateful—to our Indian princess. I might have suffered broken bones in addition to bruised flesh."

"We could not reward her," Ruth Fielding said decidedly. "I would not hurt her feelings for the world."

"We can do something nice for her, without labeling it a reward, I should hope," Helen Cameron replied. "I know what I would like to do."

"What is that?" asked Jennie, quickly.

"You remember when they dressed Wonota up in that evening frock there in New York? To take the ballroom picture, I mean?"

Alice B. Emerson

"Indeed, yes!" cried Jennie Stone. And she looked too sweet for anything."

"She is a pretty girl," agreed Ruth.

"I saw her preening before the mirror," said Helen, smiling. "That she is an Indian girl doesn't make her different from the other daughters of Eve."

"Somebody has said that the fashion-chasing women must be daughters of Lilith," put in Jennie.

"Never mind. Wonota likes pretty frocks. You could see that easily enough. And although some of the Osage girls may follow the fashions in the mail order catalogs, I believe Wonota has been brought up very simply. 'Old-fashioned,' you may say."

"Fancy!" responded Jennie. "An old-fashioned' Indian."

"I think Helen is right," said Ruth, quietly. "Wonota would like to have pretty clothes, I am sure."

"Then," said Helen, with more animation, "let us chip in—all three of us—and purchase the very nicest kind of an outfit for Wonota—a real party dress and 'all the fixin's,' girls! What say?"

"I vote 'Aye!'" agreed Jennie.

"The thought is worthy of you, Helen," said Ruth proudly. "You always do have the nicest ideas. And I am sure it will please Wonota to be dressed as were some of the girls we saw in the audiences at the theatres we took her to."

"But!" ejaculated Jennie Stone, "we can't possibly get that sort of clothes out of a mail-order catalog."

"I know just what we can do, Jennie. There is your very own dressmaker—that Madame Jone you took me to."

"Oh! Sure! Mame Jones, you mean!" cried the fleshy girl with enthusiasm. "Aunt Kate has known Mame since she worked as an apprentice with some Fifth Avenue firm. Now Madame Jone goes to Paris—when there is no war on—twice a year. She will do anything I ask her to."

"That is exactly what I mean," Helen said. "It must be some-body who will take an interest in Wonota. Send your Madame Jone a photograph of Wonota—"

"Several of them," exclaimed Ruth, interested as well, although personally she did not care so much for style as her chums. "Let the dressmaker get a complete idea of what Wonota looks like."

"And the necessary measurements," Helen said. "Give her *carte blanche* as to goods and cost—"

"Would that be wise?" interposed the more cautious Ruth.

"Leave it to me!" exclaimed Jennie Stone with confidence. "We shall have a dandy outfit, but Mame Jones will not either overcharge us or make Wonota's frock and lingerie too *outre*."

"It win be fine!" declared Helen.

"I believe it will," agreed the girl of the Red Mill.

"It will be nothing less than a knock-out," crowed Jennie, slangily.

The three friends had plenty of topics of conversation besides new frocks for Ruth's Indian star. The work of making the scenes of the prologue of "Brighteyes" went on apace, and although they all escaped acting in any of the scenes, they watched most of them from the sidelines.

Mr. Hooley had found a bright little girl (although she had no Indian blood in her veins) to play the part of the sick child in the Indian wigwam. These shots were taken in a big hay barn near the special car standing at Clearwater, and with the aid of the electric plant that had been set up here the "interiors" were very promising.

Several other "sets" were built in this make-shift studio, for all the scenes were not out-of-door pictures. The prologue scenes, however, aside from the interior of the chief's lodge, were made upon the open plain on the Hubbell Ranch not more than ten miles from the Clearwater station. Two weeks were occupied in this part of the work, for outside scenes are not shot as rapidly as those in a well equipped studio. When these were done the company moved much farther into the hills. They were to make the remaining scenes of "Brighteyes" in the wilderness, far from any human habitation more civilized than a timber camp.

Benbow Camp lay well up behind Hubbell Ranch, yet in a well sheltered valley where scarcely a threat of winter had yet appeared. A big crew of lumbermen was at work on the site, and many of these men Mr. Hammond used as extras in the scenes indicated in Ruth's script.

Ruth had now gained so much experience in the shooting of outdoor scenes that her descriptions in this story of "Brighteyes," the Indian maid, were easily visualized by the director. Besides, she stood practically at Jim Hooley's elbow when the story was being filmed. So, with the author working with the director, the picture was almost sure to be a success. At least, the hopes of all—including those of Mr. Hammond, who had already put much money into the venture—began to rise like the quicksilver in a thermometer on a hot day.

The small river on which locations had been arranged for was both a boisterous and a picturesque stream. There were swift rapids ("white water" the woodsmen called it) with outthrust boulders and many snags and shallows where a canoe had to be very carefully handled. Several scenes as Ruth had written them were of the Indian girl in a canoe. Wonota handled a paddle with the best of the rivermen at Benbow Camp. There was no failure to be feared as to the picture's requirements regarding the Indian star, at least.

Having seen the scenes of the prologue shot and got the company on location at Benbow Camp, Mr. Hammond went back to the railroad to get into communication with the East. He had other business to attend to besides the activities of this one company.

Scenes along the bank and at an Indian camp set up in a very beautiful spot were shot while preparations for one of the big scenes on the stream itself were being made.

The text called for a freshet on the river, in which the Indian maid is caught in her canoe. The disturbed water and the trash being borne down by the current was an effect arranged by Jim Hooley's workmen. The timbermen working for the Benbow Company helped.

A boom of logs was chained across the river at a narrow gorge. This held back for two nights and a day the heavy cultch floating down stream, and piled up a good deal of water, too, for the boom soon became a regular dam. Below the dam thus made the level of the stream dropped perceptibly.

"I am going to put Wonota in her canoe into the stream

Alice B. Emerson

above the boom," Hooley explained. "When the boom is cut the whole mass will shoot down ahead of the girl. But the effect, as it comes past the spot where the cameras are being cranked, will be as though Wonota was in the very midst of the freshet. She handles her paddle so well that I do not think she will be in any danger."

"But you will safeguard her, won't you, Mr. Hooley?" asked Ruth, who was always more or less nervous when these "stunt pictures" were being taken.

"There will be two canoes—and two good paddlers in each —on either side of Wonota's craft, but out of the camera focus of course. Then, we will line up a lot of the boys along the shore on either side. If she gets a ducking she won't mind. She understands. That Indian girl has some pluck, all right," concluded the director with much satisfaction.

"Yes, Wonota's courageous," agreed Ruth quietly.

Arrangements were made for the next morning. Ruth went with Mr. Hooley to the bunkhouse to hear him instruct the timbermen hired from the Benbow Company and who were much interested in this "movie stuff."

The girl of the Red Mill had already made some acquaintances among the rough but kindly fellows. She stepped into the long, shed-like bunkhouse to speak to one of her acquaintances, and there, at the end of the plank table, partaking of a late supper that the cook had just served him, was no other than Dakota Joe Fenbrook, the erstwhile proprietor of the Wild West and Frontier Round-Up.

CHAPTER XVIII

AN ACCIDENT THREATENING

Probably the ex-showman was not as surprised to see Ruth Fielding as she was to see him. But he was the first, nevertheless, to speak.

"Ho! so it's you, is it?" he growled, scowling at the girl of the Red Mill. "Reckon you didn't expect to see me."

"I certainly did not," returned Ruth tartly. "What are you doing at Benbow Camp, Mr. Fenbrook?"

"I reckon you'd be glad to hear that I walked here," sneered the showman, and filled his cheek with a mighty mouthful. He wolfed this down in an instant, and added, with a wide grin: "But I didn't. I saved my horse an' outfit from the smash, and enough loose change to bring me West—no thanks to you."

"I am sorry to hear you have failed in business, Mr. Fenbrook," Ruth said composedly. "But I am sorrier to see that you consider me in a measure to blame for your misfortune."

"Oh, don't I, though!" snarled Dakota Joe. "I know who to thank for my bust-up—you and that Hammond man.

Yes, sir-ree!"

"You are quite wrong," Ruth said, calmly. "But nothing I can say will convince you, I presume."

"You can't soft-sawder me, if that's what you mean," and Dakota Joe absorbed another mighty mouthful.

Ruth could not fail to wonder if he ever chewed his food. He seemed to swallow it as though he were a boa-constrictor.

"I know," said Dakota Joe, having swallowed the mouthful and washed it down with half a pannikin of coffee, "that you two takin' that Injun gal away from me was the beginning of my finish. Yes, sir-ree! I could ha' pulled through and made money in Chicago and St. Louis, and all along as I worked West this winter. But no, you fixed me for fair."

"Wonota had a perfect right to break with you, Mr. Fenbrook," Ruth said decidedly, and with some warmth. "You did not treat her kindly, and you paid her very little money."

"She got more money than she'd ever saw before. Them Injuns ain't used to much money. It's jest as bad for 'em as hootch. Yes, sir-ree!"

"She was worth more than you gave her. And she certainly was worthy of better treatment. But that is all over. Mr. Hammond has her tied up with a hard and fast contract. Let her alone, Mr. Fenbrook."

"Aw, don't you fret," growled the man. "I ain't come out here to trouble Wonota none. The little spitfire! She'd shoot me just as like's not if she took the notion. Them redskins ain't to be trusted—none of 'em. I know 'em only too well."

Ruth went out of the shack almost before the man had ceased speaking. She did not want anything further to do with him. She was exceedingly sorry that Dakota Joe had appeared at Benbow Camp just when the moving picture company was getting to work on the important scenes of "Brighteyes." Besides, she felt a trifle anxious because Mr. Hammond himself did not chance to be here under the present circumstances. He might be better able to handle Dakota Joe if the ruffian made trouble.

She said nothing to Jim Hooley about Dakota Joe. She did not wish to bother the director in any case. She had come to appreciate Hooley as, in a sense, a creative genius who should have his mind perfectly free of all other subjects—especially of annoying topics of thought—if he was to turn out a thoroughly good picture. Hooley fairly lived in the picture while the scenes were being shot. He must not be troubled by the knowledge of the possibility of Dakota Joe's being at Benbow Camp for some ulterior purpose.

Ruth told the girls about the man's appearance when she returned to the shacks where the members of the moving picture company were spending the night. And she warned Wonota in particular, and in private.

"He is as angry with us as he can be," the girl of the Red Mill told the Osage maiden. "I think, if I were you, Wonota, I would beware of him."

"Beware of Dakota Joe?" repeated Wonota.

"Yes."

"I would beware of him? I would shoot him?" said the Osage girl with suddenly flashing eyes. "That is what you mean?"

Ruth laughed in spite of her anxiety. "Beware" was plainly a

Alice B. Emerson

word outside the Indian girl's vocabulary.

"Don't talk like a little savage," she admonished Wonota, more severely than usual. "Of course you are not to shoot the man. You are just to see that he does you no harm—watch out for him when he is in your vicinity."

"Oh! I'll watch Dakota Joe all right," promised Wonota with emphasis. "Don't you worry about that, Miss Fielding. I'll watch him."

To Ruth's mind it seemed that the ex-showman, in his anger, was likely to try to punish the Indian girl for leaving his show, or to do some harm to the picture-making so as to injure Mr. Hammond. He had already (or so Ruth believed) endeavored to hurt Ruth herself when she was all but run over in New York. Ruth did not expect a second attack upon herself.

The next morning—the really "great day" of the picture taking—all at the camp were aroused by daybreak. There was not a soul—to the very cook of the timber-camp outfit—who was not interested in the matter. The freshet Jim Hooley had planned had to be handled in just the right way and everything connected with it must be done in the nick of time.

Wonota in her Indian canoe—a carefully selected one and decorated in Indian fashion—was embarked on the sullen stream above the timber-boom. The holding back of the water and the driftwood had formed an angry stretch of river which under ordinary circumstances Ruth and the other girls who had accompanied her West thought they would have feared to venture upon. The Indian girl, however, seemed to consider the circumstances not at all threatening.

With her on the river, but instructed to keep on either side and well out of the focus of the cameras, were two expert rivermen, each in a canoe. These men were on the alert to assist Wonota if, when the dam was broken, she should get into any difficulty.

Below the dam the men were arranged at important points, so that if the logs and drift threatened to pile up after the boom was cut, they could jump in with their pike-poles and keep the drift moving. On one shore the cameras were placed, and Jim Hooley, with his megaphone, stood on a prominent rock.

Across from the director's station Ruth found a spot at the foot of a sheer bank to the brow of which a great pile of logs had been rolled, ready for the real freshet in the spring when the log-drives would start. She had a good view of all that went on across the river, and up the stream.

Jennie suggested that she and Helen accompany Ruth and watch the taking of the picture from that vantage point, a proposal to which Helen readily agreed. But Ruth evaded this suggestion of her two friends, for she wanted to keep her whole mind on her work, and when Helen and Jennie were with her she found it impossible to keep from listening to their merry chatter, nor could she keep herself from being drawn into it. The upshot was that, after some discussion by the three girls, Ruth set off alone for her station under the brow of the steep river bank.

About ten o'clock, in mid-forenoon, Hooley was satisfied that everything was ready to shoot the picture. One of the foremen of Benbow Camp—the best ax wielder of the crew—ran out on the boom to a point near the middle of the frothing stream and began cutting the key-log. It was a ticklish piece of work; but these timbermen were used to such jobs.

The gash in the log showed wider and wider. Where Ruth stood she cocked her head to listen to the strokes of the axman. It seemed to her that there was a particularly strange echo, flattened but keen, as though reverberating from the bank of the river high above her head.

"Now, what can that be?" she thought, and once looked up the slope to the heap of logs which were held in place by chocks on the very verge of the steep descent.

If those logs should break away, Ruth realized that she was right in the path of their descent. It would not be easy for her to escape, dry-footed, In either direction, for the bank of the river, both up, and down stream, was rough.

But, of course, that chopping sound was made by the man cutting the boom. Surely nobody was using an ax up there on the pile of logs. She glanced back to the man teetering on the boom log. The gap in it was wide and white. He had cut on the down-river side. Already the pressure from up stream was forcing the gash open, wider and wider—

There came a yell from across the river. Somebody there had seen what was threatening over Ruth's head. Then Jim Hooley cast his glance that way and yelled through his megaphone:

"Jump, Miss Fielding! Quick! Jump into the river!"

But at that moment the man on the boom started for the shore, running frantically for safety. The key log split with a raucous sound. The water and drift-stuff, in a mounting wave, poured through the gap, and the noise of it deafened Ruth Fielding to all other sounds.

She did not even glance back and above again at the peril which menaced her from the top of the steep bank.

CHAPTER XIX

IN DEADLY PERIL

"This stunt business," as Director Hooley called the taking of such pictures as this, is always admittedly a gamble. After much time and hundreds of dollars have been spent in getting ready to shoot a scene, some little thing may go wrong and spoil the whole thing.

There was nothing the matter with the director's plans on this occasion; every detail of the "freshet" had been made ready for with exactness and with prodigious regard to detail.

The foreman had cut the key log almost through and the force of the water and debris behind the boom had broken it. The man barely escaped disaster by reason of agile legs and sharp caulks on his boots.

The backed-up waters burst through. Up stream, amid the turmoil and murk of the agitated flood, rode Wonota in her canoe, directly into the focus of the great cameras. To keep her canoe head-on with the flood, and to keep it from being overturned, was no small matter. It required all the Indian girl's skill to steer clear of snags and floating logs. Besides, she must remember to register as she shot down the stream a certain emotion which would reveal to the audience her condition of mind, as told in the story.

Alice B. Emerson

Wonota did her part. She was rods above the breaking dam and she could not see, because of an overhanging tree on Ruth's side of the stream, any of that peril which suddenly threatened the white girl. Wonota was as unconscious of what imperiled Ruth as the latter was at first unknowing of the coming catastrophe.

It was Jim Hooley whom the incident startled and alarmed more than anybody else. He committed an unpardonable sin —unpardonable for a director! He forgot, when everything was ready, to order the starting of the camera. Instead he put his megaphone to his lips and shouted across to Ruth Fielding—who was not supposed to be in the picture at all:

"Jump, Miss Fielding! Quick! Jump into the river!"

And Ruth did not hear him, loudly as his voice boomed across the flood! She was deafened by the thunder of the waters and the crashing of the logs in mid-flood. Her eyes, now that she was sure the foreman was safe on the other bank, were fixed upon the bow of Wonota's canoe, just coming into sight behind the ware of foaming water and upreared, charging timbers.

It was a great sight—a wonderful sight. No real freshet could have been more awful to behold. Mr. Hooley's feat was a masterstroke!

But behind and above Ruth was a scene of disaster that held those on the opposite bank speechless—after Hooley's first mighty shout of warning. At least, all but the camera men were so transfixed by the thing that was happening above the unconscious Ruth.

Trained to their work, the camera men had been ready to crank their machines when Hooley grabbed up his mega-phone. The boom had burst, the flood poured down, and the

Indian maid's canoe came into the range of their lenses.

It was the most natural thing in the world that they should begin cranking—and this they did! Alone among all those on the far bank of the stream, the camera men were blind to Ruth's danger.

"She'll be killed!" shrieked Jennie Stone, while Helen Cameron ran to the water's edge, stretching forth her arms to Ruth as though she would seize her from across the stream.

The next moment the water flooded up around Helen's ankles. The stream was rising, and had Jennie not dragged her back, Helen would have been knee-deep in the water—perhaps have been injured herself by one of the flying logs.

Ruth was out of reach of the logs in the stream, although they charged down with mighty clamor, their ends at times shooting a dozen feet into the air, the bark stripping in ragged lengths, displaying angry gashes along their flanks. It was from that great heap of logs above, on the brink of the steep bank, that Ruth was in danger.

A fringe of low brush had hidden the foot of the logpile up there. This hedge had also hidden from the observation of the party across the stream the villains who must have deliberately knocked out the chocks which held the high pile of timbers from skidding down the slope.

Mr. Hooley had seen the logs start. Squeezed out by the weight of the pile, the lower logs, stripped of bark and squealing like living creatures started over the brink. They rolled, faster and faster, down upon the unwarned Ruth Fielding. And behind the leaders poured the whole pile, gathering speed as the avalanche made headway!

The turmoil of the river and the crashing logs would have

Alice B. Emerson

smothered the sound of the avalanche until it was upon the girl of the Red Mill. No doubt of that. But providentially Ruth flashed a glance across the stream. She saw the party there all screaming at her and waving their arms madly. Jennie was just dragging Helen back from the rising flood of the turbulent river. Ruth saw by their actions that they were trying to draw her attention to something behind her.

She swung about and looked up the almost sheer bluff.

Ruth Fielding was not lacking in quick comprehension. A single glance at the descending avalanche of logs was sufficient to make her understand the peril. She knew that she could not clear the hurtling timbers by running either up stream or down. The way was too rough. As well as Jim Hooley, she knew that escape was only possible by leaping into the river. And that chance was rather uncertain.

Ruth was dressed for the rough outdoor life she was living. She wore high, laced boots, a short skirt, knickerbockers, a blouse, and a broad-brimmed hat.

When she turned to face the turbulent stream the rocking timbers coming down with the released water almost filled the pool before the endangered girl.

Had she worn caulks on the soles of her boots, as did the foreman who had cut the boom, and been practised as he was in "running the logs," Ruth would have stood a better chance of escaping the plunging avalanche. As it was, she was not wholly helpless.

She had picked up a peavey one of the timbermen had left on this bank and was using is as a staff as she watched the "freshet" start. Warned now of the danger she was in, the girl of the Red Mill seized this staff firmly in both hands and poised herself to leap from the boulder to which she had stepped.

Only a moment did she delay—just long enough to select the most promising log in the smother of foam and water before her. Then she leaped outward, striking down with the pike-staff and sinking its sharp point in the log to which she jumped.

Behind her the timbers poured down the bluff, landed on their splintering ends on the rocks, and then—many of them—pitched their long lengths into the angry river.

The spray flew yards high. It curtained, indeed, all that occurred for the next few moments upon this side of the stream. However much the scene, arranged by Jim Hooley might need the attention of the moving picture makers, here was a greater and more dangerous happening, in which Ruth Fielding was the leading participant!

Alice B. Emerson

CHAPTER XX

GOOD NEWS

Tragedy was very dose indeed at that moment to the girl of the Red Mill. Many adventures had touched Ruth nearly; but nothing more perilous had threatened her than this.

She balanced herself on the rushing log with the help of the peavey. She was more than ordinarily sure-footed. But if the log she rode chanced to be hit by one of the falling timbers loosened from their station on top of the bluff—that would be the end of the incident, and the end of the girl as well!

Perhaps it was well that Helen and Jennie could no longer see their chum. The curtain of spray thrown up by the plunging logs from above hid the whole scene for several minutes.

Then out of the turmoil on the river shot the log on which Ruth stood, appearing marvelously to her friends on the other bank.

"Ruth! Ruth Fielding!" shrieked Helen, so shrilly that her voice really could be heard. "Are you alive?"

Ruth waved one hand. She held her balance better now. She shot a glance behind and saw Wonota in the canoe coming down the rapids amid the snags and drifting debris—a wonderful picture!

Jim Hooley, almost overcome by the shock and fright, suddenly beheld his two camera men cranking steadily—as unruffled as though all this uproar and excitement was only the usual turmoil of the studio!

"Bully, boys!" the director shouted. "Keep at it!" Then through the megaphone: "Eyes on the camera, Wonota! Your lover is in the water—you must save him! Nobody else can reach him There! He's going down again! Bend forward—look at him—at the camera! That's it! When he appears again that log is going to hit him if you do not swerve the canoe in between the log and him—There! With your paddle! Shoot the canoe in now!"

He swerved the megaphone to the men waiting on the bank: "Look out for Miss Fielding, some of you fellows. The rest of you stand ready to grab Wonota when that canoe goes over."

Again to the Indian girl: "Now, Wonota! Pitch the paddle away. Lean over—grab at his head. There it is!"

The Indian girl did as instructed, leaning so far that the canoe tipped. Mr. Hooley raised his hand. He snapped his fingers. "There! Enough!" he shouted, and the cameras stopped as the canoe canted the Indian girl headfirst into the stream. The rest of that scene would be taken in quiet water.

While the man waded in to help Wonota, Ruth reached the bank and sprang off her log before she was butted off. Helen and Jennie ran to her, and such a hullabaloo as there was for a few minutes!

Jim Hooley came striding down to the three Eastern girls,

Alice B. Emerson

flushed and with scowling brow.

"I want to know who did that?" he shouted. "No thanks to anybody but my camera men that the whole scene wasn't a fizzle. And what would Mr. Hammond have said? Who were those men, Miss Fielding?"

"What men?" asked Ruth in wonder.

"Up there on the other bank? Those that knocked the chocks out from under that heap of logs? You don't suppose that avalanche of timber started all by itself?"

"I don't know what you are talking about, Mr. Hooley," declared Ruth Fielding.

"And surely," Helen added quickly, "you do not suppose that it was her fault? She might have been killed."

"I got a glimpse of a man dodging out of the way just as that pile of logs started. I saw the flash of the sun on his ax," and the director was very much in earnest.

It was Jennie who put into words the thought that had come both to Ruth and Helen as well:

"Where is that awful Dakota Joe? He was here last night. He has tried to harm our Ruthie before. I do believe he did it!"

"Who's that?" demanded the director. "The man who had Wonota in his show?"

"Yes, Mr. Hooley. He was here last night. I spoke with him up in the bunk-house while you were telling the boys about this scene," Ruth said gravely.

"The unhung villain!" exclaimed the director. "He tried to

ruin our shot."

Jennie stared at him with open mouth as well as eyes.

"Well!" she gasped after a minute. "That is what you might call being wrapped up in one's business, sure enough! Ruined your shot, indeed! How about ruining a perfectly good girl named Ruth Fielding?"

"Oh, I beg Miss Fielding's pardon," stammered the director. "You must remember that taking such a scene as this costs the corporation a good deal of money. Miss Fielding's danger, I must say, threw me quite off my balance. If I didn't have two of the keenest camera men in the business all this," and he gestured toward the turbulent river, "would have gone for nothing."

"I can thank Mr. Hooley for what he tried to do for me," smiled Ruth. "I saw his gestures if I could not hear his voice. That was my salvation. But I believe it must have been Dakota Joe who started that avalanche of logs down upon me."

"I'll have the scoundrel looked for," promised Hooley, turning to go upstream again.

"But don't tell these rough men why you want Dakota Joe," advised the girl of the Red Mill.

"No?"

"You know how they are—even some of the fellows working for the picture company. They are pretty rough themselves. I do not want murder done because of my narrow escape."

The other girls cried out at this, but Mr. Hooley nodded understandingly.

"I get you, Miss Fielding. But I'll make it so he can't try any capers around here again. No, sir!"

The girls were left to discuss the awful peril that had threatened, and come so near to over-coming, Ruth. Helen was particularly excited about it.

"I do think, Ruth, that we should start right for home. This is altogether too savage a country. To think of that rascal *daring* to do such a thing! For of course it was Dakota Joe who started those logs to rolling."

"I can imagine nobody else doing it," confessed her chum.

"Then I think you should start East at once," repeated Helen. "Don't you think so, Jennie?"

"I'd hire a guard," said the plump girl. "This country certainly is not safe for our Ruth."

"Neither was New York, it seemed," rejoined Ruth, with a whimsical smile. "Of course we are not sure—"

"We are sure you came near losing your life," interrupted Helen.

"Quite so. I was in danger. But if it was Joe, he has run away, of course. He will not be likely to linger about here after making the attempt."

And to this opinion everybody else who knew about it agreed. A search was made by some of the men for Dakota Joe. It was said he had left for another logging camp far to the north before daybreak that very morning. Nobody had seen him since that early hour.

"Just the same, he hung around long enough to start those

logs to rolling. And I am not sure but that he had help," Jim Hooley said, talking the matter over later, after Mr. Hammond had arrived from the railroad and had been told about the incident, "He is a dangerous fellow, that Fenbrook."

"He has made himself a nuisance," agreed Mr. Hammond. "Tell William and the other boys to keep their eyes open for him. The moment he appears again—if he does appear—let them grab him. I will get a warrant sworn out at Clearwater for his arrest. We will put him in jail until our picture is finished, at least."

They did not believe at the time that Ruth was in any further peril from Dakota Joe. As for the girls, they were particularly excited just then by some news Mr. Hammond had brought with him from the post-office.

Letters from Tom Cameron! He was coming home! Indeed, he would have started before Ruth and Helen received the messages he wrote. And in Ruth's letter he promised a great surprise. What that surprise was the girl of the Red Mill could not imagine.

"Doesn't he say anything about a surprise for me?" demanded Jennie Stone.

"He doesn't say a word about you in my letter, Heavy," said Helen wickedly.

"Why, Jennie, he doesn't know you are with us here in the West," Ruth said soothingly.

"I don't care," sputtered the fat girl. "He must know about my Henri. And not a word have I heard from or about him in a month. If the war is over, surely Henri must be as free as Tom Cameron."

Alice B. Emerson

"I suppose some of the soldiers have to stay along the Rhine, Jennie, dear," replied Ruth. "Maybe Henri is one of those guarding the frontier."

"He is holding the German hordes back, single-handed, from *la belle* France," put in Helen, smiling.

"Oh, cat's foot!" snapped Jennie. "The Germans are just as glad to stop fighting as we are. They certainly don't need Henri in the army any longer. I am going to write to his mother!"

CHAPTER XXI

A BULL AND A BEAR

Wonota had known nothing of what was supposed to have been a deliberate attempt to injure Ruth Fielding until some hours after the occurrence. She had not much to say about it, but, like the three white girls, she was sure the guilty man was Dakota Joe.

As William had said, Fenbrook was a "mighty mean man," and the Osage maid knew that to be a fact. She nodded her head gravely as she commented upon the incident that might have ended so seriously.

"That Dakota Joe is bad. Chief Totantora would have sent him to the spirit land long since, had he been here. There are white men, Miss Fielding, who are much worse than any redman."

"I will grant you that," sighed Ruth. "Badness is not a matter of blood, I guess. This Fenbrook has no feeling or decency. He is dangerous."

"I should have shot him," declared the Osage girl confidently. "I am afraid I have done wrong in not doing so before."

Alice B. Emerson

"How can you talk so recklessly!" exclaimed Ruth, and she was really troubled. "Shooting Dakota Joe would make you quite as bad as he is. No, no! That is not the way to feel about it."

But Wonota could not understand this logic.

And yet, Wonota in other ways was not at all reckless or ferocious. She possessed a fund of sympathy, and was kindly disposed toward everybody When one of the cook's helpers cut his foot with an ax, she aided in the rough surgery furnished by the camp boss, and afterwards nursed the invalid while he was confined to his bunk and could not even hop about.

All the men liked her, and after a time they did not speak carelessly of her as "that Injun gal." She seemed to be of a different caliber from the other Indians engaged in making the picture. At least, she was more intelligent.

The girls from the East did not lose their personal interest in Wonota in the least degree. But of course while the various scenes were being made even Ruth did not give all her attention to either the Indian maiden or to the shooting of the picture.

The great freshet scene, when developed and tried out in the projection room at Clearwater, proved to be a very striking film indeed. If "Brighteyes" was to rise to the level of that one scene, every reel of the picture must be photographed with great care.

While the director and Mr. Hammond and the company in general worked over some of the lumber-camp scenes, retaking or arranging for the shots over and over again, Ruth rode with her two chums on many a picturesque trail around Benbow Camp, Hubbell Ranch and the Clearwater station of the railroad.

They were quite sure that Dakota Joe Fenbrook had left this part of the country—and left in a hurry. If he learned that his attempt on Ruth Fielding's life was not successful, he must have learned it some time after the occurrence. Just where the "bad man" had gone after leaving Benbow on the run, nobody seemed to know.

Ruth and Helen and Jennie were in the saddle almost every day. They found much to interest them on the various trails they followed. They even discovered and visited several pioneer families—"nesters" in the language of the cowpunchers and stockmen—who welcomed the Eastern girls with vast curiosity.

"And how some of these folks can live in such Wild places, and in such perfectly barren cabins, I do not see," groaned Helen Cameron after a visit to one settler's family near a wild canyon to the west of Benbow Camp. "That woman and those girls! Not a decent garment to their backs, and the men so rough and uncouth. I would not stay there on a bet—not for the best man who ever breathed."

"That woman's husband isn't the best man who ever breathed," said Jennie, grimly. "But perhaps he is the best man she ever knew. And, anyway, having as the boys say 'got stuck on him,' now she is plainly 'stuck with him.' In other words she has made her own bed and must lie in it."

"Why should people be punished for their ignorance?" complained Helen.

"Nature's way," said Ruth confidently. "Civilization is slowly changing that—or trying to. But nature's law is, after all, rather harsh to us."

"If I was one of those girls we saw back there," Helen continued, "I would run away."

"Run where?" asked Ruth slyly. "With a movie company? Or a Wild West Show?"

"Either. Anything would be better than that hut and the savagery of their present lives."

"They don't mind it so much," admitted Jennie. "I asked one of them. She was looking forward to a dance next week. She said they had three of four through the year—and they seemed to be reckoned as great treats, but all a girl could expect."

"And think how much we demand," said Ruth thoughtfully. "Welladay! Maybe we have too much—too much of the good things of the earth."

"Bah!" exclaimed Helen, with disgust. "One can't get too much of the good things. No, ma'am! Take all you can—"

"And give nothing?" suggested Ruth, shaking her head.

"Nobody can say with truth that you are selfish, Ruthie Fielding," put in Jennie. "In fact, you are always giving, and never taking."

Ruth laughed at this. "You are wrong," she said. "The more you give the more you get. At least, I find it so. And we are getting right now, on this trip to the great Northwest, much more than we are giving. I feel as though I would be condemned if I did not do something for these hard-working people who are doing their part in developing this country— the settlers, and even the timbermen."

"You want to be a lady Santa Claus to that bunch of

roughnecks at Benbow Camp, do you?" laughed Jennie.

"Well, I would like to help somebody besides Wonota. What do you hear from your New York dressmaker about Wonota's new outfit, Jennie?"

"It will be shipped right out here to Clearwater before long," announced the plump girl, with new satisfaction. "Won't Wonota be surprised?"

"And delighted!" added Helen, showing satisfaction too.

At that very moment they rode out of a patch of wood which had hidden from the girls' eyes a piece of lowland fringed by a grove of northern cottonwood trees. On the air was borne a deep bellow—a sound that none of the three had noted before.

"What is that?" demanded Helen, startled and half drawing in her snorting pony.

"Oh, listen!" cried Jennie. "Hear the poor cow."

Ruth was inclined to doubt. "When you hear a 'cow' bellowing in this country, look out. It may be a wild steer or a very ugly bull. Let us go on cautiously."

All three of the ponies showed signs of trepidation, and this fact added to Ruth's easily aroused anxiety.

"Have a care," she said to Helen and Jennie. "I believe something is going on here that spells danger—for us at least."

"It's down in the swamp. See the way the ponies look," agreed Jennie.

They quickly came to a break in the cottonwood grove on the

Alice B. Emerson

edge of the morass. Instantly the ponies halted, snorting again. Ruth's tried to rear and turn, but she was a good horsewoman.

"Oh, look!" squealed Helen. "A bear!"

"Oh, look!" echoed Jennie, quite as excited. "A bull!"

"Well, I declare!" exclaimed Ruth, her hands full for the moment with the actions of her mount. "One would think you were looking at a picture of Wall Street—with your bulls and your bears I Let me see—do!"

CHAPTER XXII

IN THE CANYON

Ruth wheeled her mount the next moment and headed it again in the right direction. She saw at last what had caused her two companions such wonder.

In a deep hole near the edge of the morass was a huge Hereford bull. Most of the cattle in that country were Herefords.

The animal had without doubt become foundered in the swamp hole; but that was by no means the worst that had happened to him. While held more than belly-deep in the sticky mud he had been attacked by the only kind of bear in all the Rockies that, unless under great provocation, attacks anything bigger than woodmice.

A big black bear had flung itself upon the back of the bellowing, struggling bull and was tearing and biting the poor creature's head and neck—actually eating the bull by piecemeal!

"Oh, horrors!" gasped Helen, sickened by the sight of the blood and the ferocity of the bear. "Is that a dreadful grizzly? How terrible!"

Alice B. Emerson

"It's eating the poor bull alive!" Jennie cried.

Ruth had never ridden out from camp since Dakota Joe's last appearance without carrying a light rifle in her saddle scabbard. She rode a regular stockman's saddle and liked the ease and comfort of it.

Now she seized her weapon and cocked It.

"That is not a grizzly, girls!" she exclaimed. "The grizzly is ordinarily a tame animal beside this fellow. The blackbear is the meat-eater—and the man-killer, too. I learned all about that in our first trip out here to the West."

"Quick! Do something for that poor steer!" begged Helen. "Never mind lecturing about it."

But Ruth had been wasting no time while she talked. She first had to get her pony to stand She knew it was not gun-shy. It was only the scent and sight of the bear that excited it.

Once the pony's four feet were firmly set, the girl of the Red Mill, who was no bad shot, raised her rifle and sighted down the barrel at the little snarling eyes of Bruin behind his open, red jaws. The bear crouched on the bull's back and actually roared at the girls who had come to disturb him at his savage feast.

Ruth's trigger-finger was firm. It was an automatic rifle, and although it fired a small ball, the girl had drawn a good bead on the bear's most vulnerable point—the base of his wicked brain! The several bullets poured into that spot, severing the vertebrae and almost, indeed, tearing the head from the brute's shoulders!

"Oh, Ruth! You've done for him!" cried Helen, with delight.

"But the poor bull!" murmured Jennie. "See! He can't get out. He's done for."

"I am afraid they are both done for," returned Ruth. "Take this gun, Jennie. Let me see if I can rope the bull and help him out."

She swung the puncher's lariat she carried hung from her saddle-bow with much expertness. She had practised lariat throwing on her previous trips to the West. But although she was able to encircle the bull's bleeding head with the noose of the rope, to drag the creature out of the morass was impossible.

He was sunk in the mire too deeply, and he was too far gone now to help himself. The bear had rolled off the back of the bull and after a few faint struggles ceased to live. But Bruin's presence made it very difficult for the girls to force their ponies closer to the dying bull.

Therefore, after all, Ruth had to abandon her lariat, tying the end of it to a tree and by this means keeping the bull from sinking out of sight after she had put a merciful bullet into him.

As they rode near the Hubbell Ranch they stopped and told of their adventure at the swamp, and a party of the boys rode out and saved both bear and bull meat from the coyotes or from cougars that sometimes came down from the hills.

The three girls had not been idly riding about the country during these several days which had been punctuated, as it were, with the adventure of the bull and the bear. That very day they had found the canyon which Mr. Hammond and the director had been hoping to find and use in filming some of the most thrilling scenes of "Brighteyes."

Alice B. Emerson

As Ruth was the writer of the scenario it was natural that she should be quite capable of choosing the location. The lovely and sheltered canyon offered all that was needed for the taking of the scenes indicated.

The girls went back the next day, taking Mr. Hammond with them. This time they merely glanced at the spot where the bear and the bull had died, and they did not visit the family of nesters at all. The shadowy mouth of the canyon, its sides running up steeply into the hills, was long in sight before the little cavalcade reached it.

From the mouth of it Mr. Hammond could not judge if Ruth's selection of locality was a wise one. Certain natural attributes were necessary to fit the needs of the story she had written. When, after they had ridden a couple of miles up the canyon, he saw the cliff path and the lip of the overhanging rock on which the hero of the story and *Brighteyes*' Indian lover were to struggle, he proclaimed himself satisfied.

"You've got it, I do believe," the producer declared. "This will delight Jim Hooley, I am sure. We can stake out a net down here under that rock so if either or both the boys fall, they will land all right. It will be some stunt picture, and no mistake!"

He wanted to look around the place, however, before riding back, and the girls dismounted too. The bottom of the canyon was a smooth lawn—the grass still green. For although the tang of winter was now in the air even at noon, the weather had been remarkably pleasant. Only on the distant heights had the snow fallen, and not much there.

There was a silvery stream wandering through the meadow over which the girls walked. By one pool was a shallow bit of beach, and Ruth, coming upon this alone, suddenly cried out:

"Oh, Helen! Jennie! I am a Miss Crusoe. Come here and see the unmistakable mark of my Man Friday."

"What do you mean, you ridiculous thing?" drawled Jennie. "You cannot be a Crusoe. You are not dressed in skins."

"Well, I like that!" rejoined Ruth, raising her eyebrows in apparent surprise, "I should think I was covered with skin. Why not? Am I different from the remainder of humanity?"

Of course they laughed with her as they came to view her discovery upon the sand. It was the mark of a human foot.

"And no savage, I'll be bound," said Helen. "That is the mark of a mighty brogan. A white man's foot-covering, no less. See! There is another footprint."

"He certainly was going away from here," Jennie Stone observed. "Who do you suppose he is?"

"I wonder if his eyes are blue and if he has a moustache?" queried Helen, languishingly.

"Bet he has whiskers and chews tobacco. I known these Western men. Bah!"

"Jennie takes all the romance out of it," said Ruth, laughing. "Now I don't care to meet my Man Friday at all."

They ate a picnic lunch before they rode out of the lovely canyon. Mr. Hammond was always good company, and he exerted himself to be interesting to the three girls on this occasion.

"My!" Helen remarked to Jennie, "Ruth does make the nicest friends, doesn't she? See how much fun—how many good times—we have had through her acquaintanceship with

Alice B. Emerson

Mr. Hammond."

Jennie agreed. But her attention was attracted just then to something entirely different. She was staring up the cliff path that Mr. Hammond had praised as being just the natural landmark needed for the scene the company wished to picture.

"Did you see what I saw?" drawled the plump girl. "Or am I thinking too, too much about mankind?"

"What is the matter with you?" demanded Helen. "I didn't see any man."

"Not up that rocky way—there! A brown coat and a gray hat. Did you see?"

"Ruth's Man Friday!" ejaculated Helen.

"I shouldn't wonder. But we can't prove it because we haven't the size of yonder gentleman's boot. Humph I he is running away from us, all right."

"Maybe he never saw us," suggested Helen.

They called to Ruth and told her of the glimpse they had had of the stranger.

"And what did he run away for, do you suppose?" demanded Jennie.

"I am sure you need not ask me," said Ruth. "What did he look like?"

"I did not see his face," said Jennie. She repeated what she had already said to Helen about the stranger's gray hat and brown coat.

Ruth looked somewhat troubled and made no further comment Of course, the coat and hat were probably like the coat and hat of numberless other men in the West. But the last time Ruth had seen Dakota Joe Fenbrook, that individual had been wearing a broad-brimmed gray sombrero and a brown duck coat.

Alice B. Emerson

CHAPTER XXIII

REALITY

Ruth Fielding was not a coward. She had already talked so much about Dakota Joe that she was a little ashamed to bring up the subject again. So she made no comment upon the man in the brown coat and gray hat that Jennie Stone declared she had seen climbing the path up the canyon wall.

Mr. Hammond was not annoyed by it. His mind was fixed upon the scenes that could be filmed in the canyon. Like Jim Hooley, the director, his thought was almost altogether taken up with the making of Ruth's "Brighteyes."

The work of making the picture was almost concluded. Wonota, the Indian maid, had lost none of her interest in the tasks set her; but she expressed herself to Ruth as being glad that there was little more to do.

"I do not like some things I have to do," she confessed. "It is so hard to look, as Mr. Hooley tells me to, at that hero of yours, Miss Fielding, as though I admired him."

"Mr. Grand? You do not like him?"

"I could never love him," said the Indian girl with confidence. "He is too silly. Even when we are about to engage in one of the most thrilling scenes, he looks first in the hand-glass to see if his hair is parted right."

Ruth could not fail to be amused. But she said cautiously:

"But think how he would look to the audience if his hair was tousled when it was supposed to be well brushed."

"Ah, it is not a manly task," said Wonota, with disgust. "And the Indian man who is the villain—Tut! He is only half Indian. And he tries to look both as though he admired me and hated the white man. It makes his eyes go this way!" and Wonota crossed her eyes until Ruth had to cry out.

"Don't!" she begged, "Suppose you suffered that deformity?"

"But he doesn't—that Jack Onehorse. Your Brighteyes, I am sure, would have felt no pity for such an Indian."

"You don't have to feel pity for him," laughed Ruth. "You know, you shoot him in the end, Wonota."

"Most certainly," agreed Wonota, closing her lips firmly. "He deserves shooting."

The calm way in which the Indian girl spoke of this taking off of the Indian lover who became the villain in the end of the moving picture, rather shocked the young author.

"But," said Jennie, "Wonota it only a single generation removed from arrant savagery. She calls a spade a spade. You shouldn't blame her. It is civilization—which is after all a sort of make-believe—that causes us white folk to refer to a spade as an agricultural implement."

But Ruth would not laugh. She had become so much interested in Wonota by this time that she wished her to

Alice B. Emerson

improve her opportunities and learn the ways—the better ways, at least—of white people.

Mr. Hammond naturally looked at the commercial end of Wonota's improvement. Nor did Ruth overlook the chance the Osage maid had of becoming a money-earning star in the moving picture firmament. But she desired to help the girl to something better than mere money.

Wonota responded to a marked degree to Ruth's efforts. She was naturally refined. The Indian is not by nature coarse and crude. He is merely different from the whites. Wonota seemed to select for herself, when she had the opportunity, the better things obtainable—the better customs of the whites rather than the ruder ones.

Meanwhile the work of preparing for the scenes of "Brighteyes" to be shot in the canyon went on. The day came when all the company were informed that the morrow would see the work begun. At daybreak, after a hasty breakfast, the motors and vans and the cavalcade of riders left the Clearwater station for a week—and that the last week of their stay—up in the lovely canyon Ruth and her two girl chums had found.

"I do declare!" exclaimed the gay Jennie (even the lack of letters from Henri Marchand could not quench her spirits for long), "this bunch of tourists does look like an old-time emigrant train. We might be following the Santa Fe Trail, all so merrily."

"Only there were no motor-cars in those old days," remarked Ruth.

"Nor portable stoves," put in Helen with a smile.

"And I am quite sure," suggested Mr. Hammond, who heard

this, "that no moving picture cameras went along with the old Santa Fe Trailers."

"Yet," said Ruth thoughtfully, "the country about here, at any rate, is just about as wild as it was in those old days. And perhaps some of the people are quite as savage as they were in the old days. Oh, dear!"

"Who are you worrying about? William?" asked Helen slyly. "He did sound savage this morning when he was harnessing those mules to the big wagon."

But her chum did not reply to this pleasantry. She really had something on her mind which bothered her. But she did not explain the cause of her anxiety to the others, even after the arrival of the party in the canyon.

It looked like a great Gypsy camp when the party was settled on the sward beside the mountain stream. Mr. Hooley had not seen the location before, and he was somewhat critical of some points. But finally he admitted that, unless the place had been built for their need, they could not really expect to find a location better fitted.

"And thank goodness!" Ruth sighed, when the camera points were severally decided upon, "after these shots are taken we can head East for good."

"Why, Ruthie! I thought we were having a dandy time," exclaimed Helen. "Have you lost your old love for the wild and open places?"

"I certainly will be glad to see a porcelain bathtub again," yawned Jennie, breaking in. "I don't really feel as though a sponge-down in an icy cold brook with a tarpaulin around one for a bath-house is altogether the height of luxury."

"It is out here," laughed Helen.

"I do not mind the inconveniences so much," said Ruth reflectively. "The old Red Mill farmhouse was not very conveniently arranged—above stairs, at least—until I had it built over at my own expense, greatly to Uncle Jabez's opposition. It is not the roughing it. That is good for us I verily believe. But I have a depressing feeling that before the picture is done something may happen."

"I should expect it would!" cried Helen, not at all disturbed by the prophecy. Once Helen had prophesied disaster, and it had come. But she forgot that now. "I expect something to happen—every day, most likely. But of course it will be a pleasant and exciting something. Yes, indeedy!"

Neither of her friends, after all, realized that Ruth Fielding was actually in fear. She was very anxious every waking moment. That strange man whom the girls had spied here in the canyon might be a perfectly harmless person. And then again—

Two days were occupied in placing the paraphernalia and training the actors in their parts. They all got a working knowledge of what was expected of them when the picture was being photographed, and the principals learned their lines. For nowadays almost as much care is given to what is said by actors before the camera as by those having speaking parts upon the stage.

The big scene—the really big scene in the drama—was set upon that overhanging lip of rock that Ruth had spied when first she, with Helen and Jennie, had ridden up the trail. On that overhanging shelf occurred the struggle between the white lover of *Brighteyes* and the Indian who had trailed him and the girl to this wild spot.

Mr. Grand, in spite of Wonota's scorn of him, was a handsome man and made as fine an appearance in the out-of-door garments the part called for as he did in the dress-suit to which he was so much addicted. The Indian who played the part of the villain was an excellent actor and had appeared many times on the silver sheet. He was earnest in his desire to please the director, but he failed sometimes to "keep in the picture" when he was not actually dominating a scene.

Because of this failing in John Onehorse, Mr. Hooley sent Ruth to the top of the rock to watch and advise Onehorse as the scene proceeded.

She was quite able by this time to act as assistant director. Indeed, it was Ruth's ambition to direct a picture of her own in the near future. She sometimes had ideas that conflicted with those of Mr. Hammond and his directors, and she wished to try her own way to get certain results.

Now, however, she was to follow Mr. Hooley's instructions exactly.

The arrangement of the cameras were such, both from below and at the level of the scene to be shot, that Ruth had to stand upon a narrow shelf quite out of sight of the actors on the overhanging rock, and hidden as well from most of the people below. This, to make sure that she was out of the line of the camera.

Behind her the narrow and broken trail led to the top of the canyon wall. It was up this trail that Jennie and Helen had seen the "Man Friday" disappear on the occasion of their first visit to the place.

Patiently, over and over again, Mr. Hooley had the principal characters try the scene. Below, Wonota, as the heroine, was to run into the camera field at a certain point in the struggle of the two men on the lip of rock. To time the Indian girl's entrance was no small task. But at last the characters seemed to be about letter perfect.

"Look out now! We're going to shoot it!" shouted Jim Hooley through his megaphone. "Miss Fielding! Keep your eye on Onehorse. Keep him up to the mark while he waits for Mr. Grand's speech. Now! Ready?"

It was at just this moment that Ruth felt something—something hard and painful—pressing between her shoulder-blades. She shot a glance over her shoulder to see the ugly face of Dakota Joe Fenbrook peering out at her between the walls of a narrow crack in the face of the cliff. The thing he pressed against her was a long stick, and, with a grin of menace, he drove that stick more firmly against Ruth's body!

"Ready? Camera! Go!" shouted Mr. Hooley, and the scene was on.

Ruth, with a stifled cry, realized that she was being pushed to the edge of the steep path. There was a drop of twenty feet and more, and where she stood there was no net to break the fall!

If Fenbrook pushed her over the brink of the path Ruth knew very well that the outcome would be even too realistic for a moving picture.

CHAPTER XXIV

WONOTA'S SURPRISE

Ruth Fielding might have cried out. But at that moment the attention of everyone was so given to the taking of the important scene that perhaps nobody would have understood her cry—what it meant.

Behind her Dakota Joe stretched forward, pushing the stick into the small of her back and urging her closer to the brink. The spot on which she stood was so narrow that it was impossible for her to escape without turning her body, and the bad man knew very well that the pressure of the stick kept her from doing that very thing!

The cameras were being cranked steadily, and Mr. Hooley shouted his orders as needed. Fortunately for the success of the scene, Onehorse did not need the admonitions of Ruth to "keep in the picture." The point came where he made his leap for the shoulders of the white man, and it was timed exactly. The two came to the brink of the rock in perfect accord with the appearance of Wonota on the ground below.

The Indian girl came, gun in hand, as though just from the chase. As she ran into the field of the camera Hooley shouted his advice and she obeyed his words to the letter. Until—

Alice B. Emerson

She raised her eyes, quite as she was told. But she looked beyond Grand and Onehorse struggling on the rock. It was to another figure she looked—that of Ruth being forced over the verge of the narrow path.

The girl of the Red Mill was half crouched, striving to push back against the thrust of the stick in Dakota Joe's hands. The upper part of Fenbrook's body was plainly visible from Wonota's station at the foot of the cliff, and his wicked face could be mistaken for no other.

"Now! The gun!" shouted Mr. Hooley. "Wonota! Come alive!"

The Indian girl obeyed—as far as springing into action went. The gun she held went to her shoulder, but its muzzle did not point at the actors above her. Instead, the threatening weapon pointed directly at the head of the villain who was forcing Ruth off her insecure footing on the narrow path.

"What are you doing, Wonota? Wonota!" shouted Mr. Hooley, who could not see Ruth at all.

The Indian girl made no reply. She drew bead upon the head of Dakota Joe, and his glaring eyes were transfixed by the appearance of the gaping muzzle of Wonota's gun.

He dropped the stick with which he had forced Ruth to the edge of the path. She fell sideways, dizzy and faint, clinging to the rough rock with both hands. As it was, she came near rolling over the declivity after all.

But it was Dakota Joe, in his sudden panic, who came to disaster. He had always been afraid of Wonota. She was a dead shot, and he believed that she would not shrink from killing him.

Now it appeared that the Indian girl held his life in her hands. The muzzle of her weapon looked to Dakota Joe at that moment as big as the mouth of a cannon!

He could see her brown finger curled upon the trigger. Each split second threatened the discharge of the gun.

With a stifled cry he tried to leap out of the crack and along the path down which he had come so secretly. But he stumbled. His riding boots were not fit for climbing on such a rugged shelf. Stumbling again, he threw out one hand to find nothing more stable to clutch than the empty air!

"Wonota!" shouted Hooley again. "Stop!" He raised his hand, stopping the cameras.

And at that moment there hurtled over the edge of the path a figure that, whirling and screaming, fell all the distance to the bottom of the canyon. Helen and Jennie, for a breathless instant, thought it must be Ruth, for they knew where she had been hidden. But the voice that roared fear and imprecations was not at all like Ruth Fielding's!

"Who's that?" shouted Mr. Hammond, likewise excited. "He's spoiled that shot, I am sure."

Ruth sat up on the shelf and looked over.

"Oh!" she cried. "Is he killed?"

"He ought to be, if he isn't," growled Mr. Hooley. "What did you do that for, Wonota?"

The Indian girl advanced upon the man writhing on the ground. Dakota Joe saw her coming and set up another frightened yell.

Alice B. Emerson

"Don't let her shoot me! Don't let her!" he begged.

"Shut up!" commanded Mr. Hammond. "The gun only has blanks in it. We don't use loaded cartridges in this business. Why! hanged if it isn't Fenbrook."

"Now you have busted me up!" groaned the ex-showman. "I got a broken leg. And I believe my arm's broken too. And that gal done it."

As Jennie said later, however, he could scarcely "get away with that." Ruth came down and told what the rascal had tried to do to her. For a little while it looked as though some of the rougher fellows might do the dastardly Joe bodily harm other than that caused by his fall. But Mr. Hammond hurried him in a motor-car to Clearwater, and there, before the moving picture company returned, he was tried and sent to the State penitentiary.

The great scene had to be taken over again—a costly and nerve-racking experience. Like Ruth herself, Helen and Jennie were glad now when the work was finished and they could head for the railroad.

"Guess you were right, Ruthie," agreed Jennie. "Something did happen. As Aunt Alvirah would have said, you must have felt it in your bones."

"I feel it in my body, anyway," admitted Ruth. "I got dreadfully bruised when I fell on that path. My side is all black and blue."

The misadventures of the occasion were soon forgotten however, especially when the girls reached Clearwater and found a box waiting for them at the express office. Unsuspicious Wonota was called into the stateroom in the special car, and there her white friends displayed to her delighted gaze the "trousseau," as Jennie insisted upon calling the pretty frock and other articles sent on by Madame Jone.

"For *me*?" asked Wonota, for once showing every indication of delight without being ordered to do so by the director. "All for me? Oh, it is too much! How my father, Chief Totantora, would stare could he see me in those beautiful things. Wonota's white sisters are doing too much for her. There is no way by which she can repay their kindness."

"Say!" said Jennie bluntly, "if you want to pay Ruth Fielding, you just go ahead and become a real movie star—a real Indian star, Wonota. I can see well enough that then she will get big returns on her investment. And in any case, we are all delighted that you are pleased with our present."

Alice B. Emerson

CHAPTER XXV

OTHER SURPRISES

It was not merely a matter of packing up and starting for the East. It would be a week still before the party would separate—some of the Westerners starting for California and the great moving picture studios there, while Ruth and her friends with Mr. Hammond and his personal staff would go eastward.

It had been arranged that Wonota should return to the Osage Agency for a short time. Meanwhile Ruth had promised to try to do another scenario in which the young Indian girl would have an important part.

Mr. Hammond was enthusiastic, having seen some of the principal scenes of "Brighteyes" projected. He declared to Ruth:

"She is going to be what our friend the camera man calls 'a knock-out.' There is a charm about Wonota—a wistfulness and naturalness—that I believe will catch the movie fans. Maybe, Miss Fielding, we are on the verge of making one of the few really big hits in the game."

"I think she is quite worthy of training, Mr. Hammond," agreed the girl of the Red Mill. "When I get to work on the new picture I shall want Wonota with me. Can it be arranged?"

"Surely. Her contract takes that into consideration. Unless her father appears on the scene, for the next two years Wonota is to be as much under your instruction as though she were an apprentice," and he laughed.

Mention of Chief Totantora did not warn Ruth of any pending event. The thing which happened was quite unexpected as far as she was concerned.

The westbound train halted at Clearwater one afternoon, while the three white girls were sitting on the rear platform of their car busy with certain necessary needlework—for there were no maids in the party. Ruth idly raised her eyes to see who got off the train, for the station was in plain view.

"There are two soldiers," she said. "Look! Boys coming home from 'over there,' I do believe. See! They have their trench helmets slung behind them with their other duffle. Why—"

She halted. Helen had looked up lazily, but it was Jennie who first exclaimed in rejoinder to Ruth's observation:

"Dear me, it surely isn't my Henri!"

"No," said Ruth slowly, but still staring, "there is no horizon blue uniform in sight."

"Don't remind us of such possibilities," complained Helen Cameron with a deep sigh. "If Tom—"

"It *is*!" gasped Ruth, under her breath, and suddenly the other girls looked at her to observe an almost beatific expression spread over the features of the girl of the Red Mill.

"Ruthie!" cried Helen, and jumped up from her seat.

"My aunt!" murmured Jennie, and stared as hard as she could along the beaten path toward the station.

The two figures in uniform strode toward the special car. One straight and youthful figure came ahead, while the other soldier, as though in a subservient position, followed in the first one's footsteps.

Wonota was coming across the street toward the railroad. She, too, saw the pair of uniformed men. For an instant the Indian girl halted. Then she bounded toward the pair, her light feet fairly spurning the ground.

"My father! Chief Totantora!" the white girls heard her cry.

The leading soldier halted, swung about to look at her, and said something to his companion. Not until this order was given him did the second man even look in the direction of the flying Indian maid.

Ruth and her friends then saw that he was a man past middle age, that his face was that of an Indian, and that his expression was quite as stoical as the countenances of Indians are usually presumed to be.

But Wonota had learned of late to give way to her feelings. No white girl could have flung herself into the arms of her long-lost parent with more abandon than did Wonota. And that not-withstanding the costume she wore—the very pretty one sent West from the Fifth Avenue modiste's shop!

Perhaps the change in his lovely daughter shocked Totantora at first, He seemed not at all sure that this was really his Wonota. Nor did he put his arms about her as a white father would have done. But he patted her shoulder, and then her cheek, and in earnest gutturals he conversed a long time with the Indian maid.

Meanwhile the three white girls had their own special surprise. The white soldier, who was plainly an officer, advanced toward the special car. His bronzed and smiling face was not to be mistaken even at that distance. Helen suddenly cried:

"Hold me, somebody! I know I'm going to faint! That's Tommy-boy."

Ruth, however, gave no sign of fainting. She dashed off the steps of the car and ran several yards to meet the handsome soldier. Then she halted, blushing to think of the appearance she made. Suppose members of the company should see her?

"Well, Ruth," cried the broadly smiling Tom, "is that the way you greet your best chum's brother? Say! You girls ought to be kinder than this to us. Why! when we paraded in New York an old lady ran right out into the street and kissed me."

"And how many pretty girls did the same, Captain Tom?" Ruth wanted to know sedately.

"Nobody as pretty as you, Ruth," he whispered, seizing both her hands and kissing her just as his sister and Jennie reached the spot. He let Helen—and even Jennie—kiss him also.

"You know how it is, Tommy," the latter explained. "If I can't kiss my own soldier, why shouldn't I practise on you?"

"No reason at all, Jennie," he declared. "But let me tell the good news. By the time you get back to New York a certain major in the French forces expects to be relieved and to be on his way to the States again. He tells me that you are soon going to become a French citizeness, *ma cherie.*

Alice B. Emerson

It was a very gay party that sat for the remainder of that afternoon on the observation platform of the special car. There was so much to say on both sides.

"So the appearance of Wonota's father was the great surprise you had in store for us, Tom?" Ruth said at one point.

"That's it. And some story that old fellow can tell his daughter—if he warms up enough to do it. These Indians certainly are funny people. He seems to have taken a shine to me and follows me around a good deal as though he were my servant. Yet I understand that he belongs to the very rich Osage tribe, and is really one of the big men of it."

"Quite true," Ruth said.

The story of Totantora's adventures in Germany was a thrilling one. But only by hearsay had Tom got the details. The Indians and other performers put in confinement by the Germans when the war began, had all suffered more or less. Twice Chief Totantora had escaped and tried to make his way out of the country. Each time he had been caught, and more severely treated.

The third time he had succeeded in breaking through into neutral territory. Even there, in a strange land, amid unfamiliar customs and people talking an unknown language, he had made his way alone and without help till he had reached the American lines. Perhaps one less stoical, with less endurance, than an Indian, and an Indian, like Chief Totantora, trained in an earlier, hardier day, could not have done it. But Wonota's father did succeed, and after he reached the American lines he became attached in some indefinite capacity to Captain Tom Cameron's regiment.

"When I first saw the poor old chap he was little more than a skeleton. But the life Indians lead certainly makes them tough and enduring. He stood starvation and confinement better than the white men. Some of the ex-show people died in that influenza epidemic the second year of the war. But old Totantora was pretty husky, in spite of having all the appearance of a professional living skeleton," explained Tom.

Whether Totantora told Wonota the details of his imprisonment or not, the white girls never knew. Wonota, too, was inclined to be very secretive. But she was supremely happy.

She was to have a recess from work, and when the special car started East with Ruth and her chums, Wonota and her father accompanied them to Kansas City. Then the Osages went south to the reservation.

Totantora had heard all about his daughter's work in the moving picture before the party separated, and he put his mark on Mr. Hammond's contract binding himself to allow the girl to go on as already agreed. Totantora had possibly some old-fashioned Indian ideas about the treatment of squaws; but he knew the value of money. The sums Wonota had already been paid were very satisfactory to the chief of the Osages.

In Ruth's mind, the money part of the contract was the smallest part. She desired greatly to see Wonota develop and grow in her chosen profession. To see the Indian maid become a popular screen star was going to delight the girl of the Red Mill, and she was frank in saying so.

"See here," Tom Cameron said when they were alone together. "I can see very well, Ruthie, that you are even more enamored of your profession than you were before I left for Europe. How long is this going to last?"

"How long is what going to last?" she asked him, her frank

Alice B. Emerson

gaze finding his.

"You know what I mean," said the young man boyishly. "Gee, Ruth! the war is over. You know what I want. And I feel as though I deserved some consideration after what I have been through."

She smiled, but still looked at him levelly.

"Well, how about it?" he demanded.

"Do you think we know our own minds? Altogether, I mean?" asked the girl. "You are in a dreadfully unsettled state. I can see that, Tom. And I have only just begun with Wonota. I could not stop now."

"I don't ask you to stop a single, solitary thing!" he cried with sudden heat. "I expect to get to work myself—at something. I feel a lot of energy boiling up in me," and he laughed.

"But, say, Ruth, I want to know just what I am going to work for? Is it all right with you? Haven't found anybody else you like better than your old chum, have you?"

Ruth laughed, too. Yet she was serious when she gave him both her hands.

"I am very sure, Tom, dear, that that could never be. You will always be the best beloved of all boys—"

"Great Scott, Ruth!" he interrupted. "When do you think I am going to be a man?"

THE END

Choose from Thousands of 1stWorldLibrary Classics By

A. M. Barnard	Booth Tarkington	Edward Everett Hale
Ada Leverson	Boyd Cable	Edward J. O'Biren
Adolphus William Ward	Bram Stoker	Edward S. Ellis
Aesop	C. Collodi	Edwin L. Arnold
Agatha Christie	C. E. Orr	Eleanor Atkins
Alexander Aaronsohn	C. M. Ingleby	Eleanor Hallowell Abbott
Alexander Kielland	Carolyn Wells	Eliot Gregory
Alexandre Dumas	Catherine Parr Traill	Elizabeth Gaskell
Alfred Gatty	Charles A. Eastman	Elizabeth McCracken
Alfred Ollivant	Charles Amory Beach	Elizabeth Von Arnim
Alice Duer Miller	Charles Dickens	Ellem Key
Alice Turner Curtis	Charles Dudley Warner	Emerson Hough
Alice Dunbar	Charles Farrar Browne	Emilie F. Carlen
Allen Chapman	Charles Ives	Emily Bronte
Alleyne Ireland	Charles Kingsley	Emily Dickinson
Ambrose Bierce	Charles Klein	Enid Bagnold
Amelia E. Barr	Charles Hanson Towne	Enilor Macartney Lane
Amory H. Bradford	Charles Lathrop Pack	Erasmus W. Jones
Andrew Lang	Charles Romyn Dake	Ernie Howard Pie
Andrew McFarland Davis	Charles Whibley	Ethel May Dell
Andy Adams	Charles Willing Beale	Ethel Turner
Angela Brazil	Charlotte M. Braeme	Ethel Watts Mumford
Anna Alice Chapin	Charlotte M. Yonge	Eugene Sue
Anna Sewell	Charlotte Perkins Stetson	Eugenie Foa
Annie Besant	Clair W. Hayes	Eugene Wood
Annie Hamilton Donnell	Clarence Day Jr.	Eustace Hale Ball
Annie Payson Call	Clarence E. Mulford	Evelyn Everett-green
Annie Roe Carr	Clemence Housman	Everard Cotes
Annonaymous	Confucius	F. H. Cheley
Anton Chekhov	Coningsby Dawson	F. J. Cross
Archibald Lee Fletcher	Cornelis DeWitt Wilcox	F. Marion Crawford
Arnold Bennett	Cyril Burleigh	Fannie E. Newberry
Arthur C. Benson	D. H. Lawrence	Federick Austin Ogg
Arthur Conan Doyle	Daniel Defoe	Ferdinand Ossendowski
Arthur M. Winfield	David Garnett	Fergus Hume
Arthur Ransome	Dinah Craik	Florence A. Kilpatrick
Arthur Schnitzler	Don Carlos Janes	Fremont B. Deering
Arthur Train	Donald Keyhoe	Francis Bacon
Atticus	Dorothy Kilner	Francis Darwin
B.H. Baden-Powell	Dougan Clark	Frances Hodgson Burnett
B. M. Bower	Douglas Fairbanks	Frances Parkinson Keyes
B. C. Chatterjee	E. Nesbit	Frank Gee Patchin
Baroness Emmuska Orczy	E. P. Roe	Frank Harris
Baroness Orczy	E. Phillips Oppenheim	Frank Jewett Mather
Basil King	E. S. Brooks	Frank L. Packard
Bayard Taylor	Earl Barnes	Frank V. Webster
Ben Macomber	Edgar Rice Burroughs	Frederic Stewart Isham
Bertha Muzzy Bower	Edith Van Dyne	Frederick Trevor Hill
Bjornstjerne Bjornson	Edith Wharton	Frederick Winslow Taylor

Friedrich Kerst
Friedrich Nietzsche
Fyodor Dostoyevsky
G.A. Henty
G.K. Chesterton
Gabrielle E. Jackson
Garrett P. Serviss
Gaston Leroux
George A. Warren
George Ade
Geroge Bernard Shaw
George Cary Eggleston
George Durston
George Ebers
George Eliot
George Gissing
George MacDonald
George Meredith
George Orwell
George Sylvester Viereck
George Tucker
George W. Cable
George Wharton James
Gertrude Atherton
Gordon Casserly
Grace E. King
Grace Gallatin
Grace Greenwood
Grant Allen
Guillermo A. Sherwell
Gulielma Zollinger
Gustav Flaubert
H. A. Cody
H. B. Irving
H.C. Bailey
H. G. Wells
H. H. Munro
H. Irving Hancock
H. R. Naylor
H. Rider Haggard
H. W. C. Davis
Haldeman Julius
Hall Caine
Hamilton Wright Mabie
Hans Christian Andersen
Harold Avery
Harold McGrath
Harriet Beecher Stowe
Harry Castlemon
Harry Coghill
Harry Houidini

Hayden Carruth
Helent Hunt Jackson
Helen Nicolay
Hendrik Conscience
Hendy David Thoreau
Henri Barbusse
Henrik Ibsen
Henry Adams
Henry Ford
Henry Frost
Henry James
Henry Jones Ford
Henry Seton Merriman
Henry W Longfellow
Herbert A. Giles
Herbert Carter
Herbert N. Casson
Herman Hesse
Hildegard G. Frey
Homer
Honore De Balzac
Horace B. Day
Horace Walpole
Horatio Alger Jr.
Howard Pyle
Howard R. Garis
Hugh Lofting
Hugh Walpole
Humphry Ward
Ian Maclaren
Inez Haynes Gillmore
Irving Bacheller
Isabel Cecilia Williams
Isabel Hornibrook
Israel Abrahams
Ivan Turgenev
J.G.Austin
J. Henri Fabre
J. M. Barrie
J. M. Walsh
J. Macdonald Oxley
J. R. Miller
J. S. Fletcher
J. S. Knowles
J. Storer Clouston
J. W. Duffield
Jack London
Jacob Abbott
James Allen
James Andrews
James Baldwin

James Branch Cabell
James DeMille
James Joyce
James Lane Allen
James Lane Allen
James Oliver Curwood
James Oppenheim
James Otis
James R. Driscoll
Jane Abbott
Jane Austen
Jane L. Stewart
Janet Aldridge
Jens Peter Jacobsen
Jerome K. Jerome
Jessie Graham Flower
John Buchan
John Burroughs
John Cournos
John F. Kennedy
John Gay
John Glasworthy
John Habberton
John Joy Bell
John Kendrick Bangs
John Milton
John Philip Sousa
John Taintor Foote
Jonas Lauritz Idemil Lie
Jonathan Swift
Joseph A. Altsheler
Joseph Carey
Joseph Conrad
Joseph E. Badger Jr
Joseph Hergesheimer
Joseph Jacobs
Jules Vernes
Julian Hawthrone
Julie A Lippmann
Justin Huntly McCarthy
Kakuzo Okakura
Karle Wilson Baker
Kate Chopin
Kenneth Grahame
Kenneth McGaffey
Kate Langley Bosher
Kate Langley Bosher
Katherine Cecil Thurston
Katherine Stokes
L. A. Abbot
L. T. Meade

L. Frank Baum
Latta Griswold
Laura Dent Crane
Laura Lee Hope
Laurence Housman
Lawrence Beasley
Leo Tolstoy
Leonid Andreyev
Lewis Carroll
Lewis Sperry Chafer
Lilian Bell
Lloyd Osbourne
Louis Hughes
Louis Joseph Vance
Louis Tracy
Louisa May Alcott
Lucy Fitch Perkins
Lucy Maud Montgomery
Luther Benson
Lydia Miller Middleton
Lyndon Orr
M. Corvus
M. H. Adams
Margaret E. Sangster
Margret Howth
Margaret Vandercook
Margaret W. Hungerford
Margret Penrose
Maria Edgeworth
Maria Thompson Daviess
Mariano Azuela
Marion Polk Angellotti
Mark Overton
Mark Twain
Mary Austin
Mary Catherine Crowley
Mary Cole
Mary Hastings Bradley
Mary Roberts Rinehart
Mary Rowlandson
M. Wollstonecraft Shelley
Maud Lindsay
Max Beerbohm
Myra Kelly
Nathaniel Hawthrone
Nicolo Machiavelli
O. F. Walton
Oscar Wilde

Owen Johnson
P.G. Wodehouse
Paul and Mabel Thorne
Paul G. Tomlinson
Paul Severing
Percy Brebner
Percy Keese Fitzhugh
Peter B. Kyne
Plato
Quincy Allen
R. Derby Holmes
R. L. Stevenson
R. S. Ball
Rabindranath Tagore
Rahul Alvares
Ralph Bonehill
Ralph Henry Barbour
Ralph Victor
Ralph Waldo Emmerson
Rene Descartes
Ray Cummings
Rex Beach
Rex E. Beach
Richard Harding Davis
Richard Jefferies
Richard Le Gallienne
Robert Barr
Robert Frost
Robert Gordon Anderson
Robert L. Drake
Robert Lansing
Robert Lynd
Robert Michael Ballantyne
Robert W. Chambers
Rosa Nouchette Carey
Rudyard Kipling
Saint Augustine
Samuel B. Allison
Samuel Hopkins Adams
Sarah Bernhardt
Sarah C. Hallowell
Selma Lagerlof
Sherwood Anderson
Sigmund Freud
Standish O'Grady
Stanley Weyman
Stella Benson
Stella M. Francis

Stephen Crane
Stewart Edward White
Stijn Streuvels
Swami Abhedananda
Swami Parmananda
T. S. Ackland
T. S. Arthur
The Princess Der Ling
Thomas A. Janvier
Thomas A Kempis
Thomas Anderton
Thomas Bailey Aldrich
Thomas Bulfinch
Thomas De Quincey
Thomas Dixon
Thomas H. Huxley
Thomas Hardy
Thomas More
Thornton W. Burgess
U. S. Grant
Upton Sinclair
Valentine Williams
Various Authors
Vaughan Kester
Victor Appleton
Victor G. Durham
Victoria Cross
Virginia Woolf
Wadsworth Camp
Walter Camp
Walter Scott
Washington Irving
Wilbur Lawton
Wilkie Collins
Willa Cather
Willard F. Baker
William Dean Howells
William le Queux
W. Makepeace Thackeray
William W. Walter
William Shakespeare
Winston Churchill
Yei Theodora Ozaki
Yogi Ramacharaka
Young E. Allison
Zane Grey

www.ingramcontent.com/pod-product-compliance
Lightning Source LLC
Chambersburg PA
CBHW031351170626
46807CB00002B/924